SPIRIT OF ADVENTURE

A competitor's view of the epic Peking to Paris Motor Challenge of 1997

by
BRIAN ASHBY

Published
by
Hawk Publishing Limited
The Old Vicarage
226 Ashbourne Road
Derbyshire
DE56 2LH
Tel: 01773 550173

Printed by:
Derbyshire Colour Services Ltd
6b Monk Road Industrial Estate
Alfreton
Derbyshire DE55 7RL
Tel: 01773 836677

This book is dedicated to my son and co-driver, Duncan Ashby.

⚜

The unique aspect of this book is that the reader becomes the driver of an open vintage car, competing in the longest motoring rally ever completed - the Peking to Paris Motor Challenge of 1997. Imagine yourself sitting behind the wheel as the rally commences. Your car will be one of only six vintage cars to complete the course and you will anguish over preparations, deprivation, hunger, thirst, sickness, exhaustion, the disintegration of a treasured car and penetratingly disturbing danger.

You will be warmed by the bursts of humour and comradeship, moved by the humanity, despoliation, history and beauty floating by on both sides of the car and thrilled to partake in the spirit of adventure aroused by the epic journey across Asia and Europe.

*The author with his son and co-driver, Duncan Ashby, and
his 1930 Delage D8 just prior to shipment to China*

Brian Ashby was born in Birmingham, England and is a Fellow of the Royal Institution of Chartered Surveyors. He founded his own company which grew into an international property development and investment group with four offices in Britain and North America. He is a passionate skier and a successful amateur motor-racing driver. He is married with three children and lives in Derbyshire.

PUBLISHER'S ACKNOWLEDGEMENTS

The Publishers are very grateful to the following for allowing them to re-produce
the map and the pictures in this book:

- Fritz W. Walter
- Michael Johnson
- Andrew Heading Photography
- Duncan Ashby
- Ordnance Survey

ISBN 1–900686–02–3

ACKNOWLEDGEMENTS

I offer my grateful thanks for the advice and help freely given to me regarding this book by Duncan Ashby and my wife, Irene.

I thank Lyn Stevens for co-ordinating research, word processing and reading the text also Beryl Winfield for her patience and support in proof reading the manuscript.

FOREWORD

It is not my intent to attempt to enlighten readers on issues of demography, history, geography, climate or politics. Any reference to those matters in passing is part of my wish to lead readers through the experience of actually taking part in the historic Peking to Paris Challenge of 1997 and the variety of thoughts which are aroused en route.

I would like you to feel and see the experience as though you were a driver or co-driver in a vintage, open sided, drop-head coupé.

Hang on to your hat!

PHOTOGRAPHS

Dust Sheet - Mount Ararat, Turkey

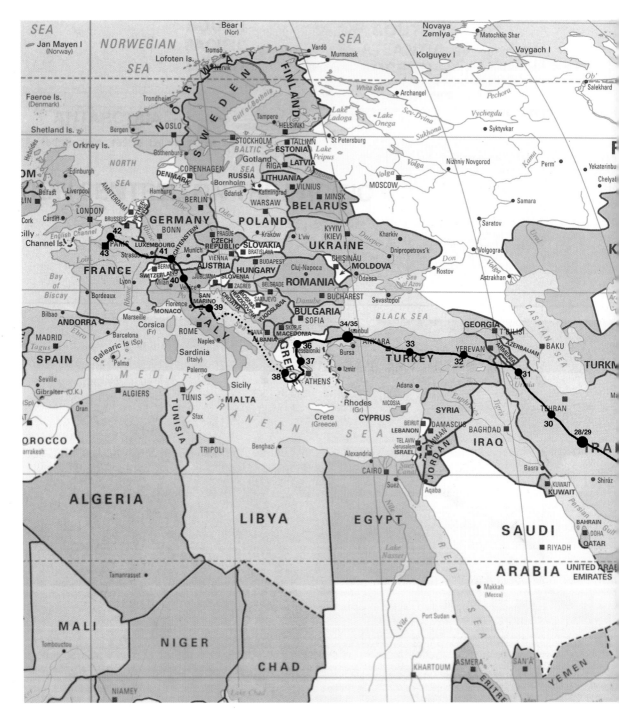

the epic

or Challenge 1997

● - *denotes each overnight stay*

Chapter

1

Is it a flaw in the human psyche that a man or a woman can decide in an instant to accept a challenge, only to discern by degrees the effort and sacrifice required to meet that challenge? The power of the human brain is widely and vastly underestimated. The production of a decision in an instant belies the scores of issues sifted and weighed by those compact lobes. No man-made computer has yet approached rivalling the human brain in the range and power of its programmes. So why does this staggeringly efficient facility often stand back from its product and re-examine the process in detail over days, weeks, months, sometimes years, until the challenge is met or conceded?

In 1995 I saw the opportunity to compete in the Peking to Paris Motor Challenge of 1997, driving my 1930 Delage D8, and in an instant I accepted that challenge. I asked my son, Duncan, if he would like to be my co-driver and without hesitation he accepted. Two years later, after endless rebuilding, restoration, testing and re-testing, [1] our vintage Delage was shipped from Felixstowe to Peking aboard the vessel, 'Feihe', which departed on 21st July, 1997.

The concept of the Challenge was to replicate the Peking to Paris Race of 1907, won by Prince Borghese in an Itala. It was the brain child of Phil Young of the Classic Rally Association, who is recognised as a capable organiser of vintage and classic motoring rallies. He accepted from the beginning that, in 1997, it would have to be a timed trial or rally rather than a race. Also, he decided that the route would have to be varied to [2] avoid modernised roads. In short, he wanted authentic road conditions in preference to finite geographical accuracy. A total of ninety four cars entered the 1997 rally, with [3] their drivers and co-drivers representing twenty six nationalities

By the beginning of 1997 we knew that we would have to nurse our vintage car over a period of forty three days through sixteen thousand kilometres of enormously varied terrain. It would include driving on the highest road in the world - 'the Roof of the World' - through the Himalayas, and reaching a height of 17,000 ft. To put it in perspective, that is 3,500 ft higher than the world famous, permanently snow-capped Matterhorn in Zermatt. We decided that we would have to be prepared to change the

[1] The full restoration is listed in Appendix 1
[2] See route map prior to page 1
[3] Entrants listed in Appendix 2

needles in the carburettors at say, 10,000 ft to allow for the reduced oxygen between 10,000 ft and 17,000 ft. We knew that our own bodies could be adversely affected by this lack of oxygen. We might avoid complications if we were able to drive smoothly through the highest altitude but if, for example, we had to change a wheel, we might suffer dizziness and altitude sickness. We decided to take a small oxygen unit for each of us. Each small unit gave a mere eighty puffs of oxygen. What was really needed was a full oxygen cylinder but we simply did not have room for it.

We also learnt that there were no less than thirteen rivers to be forded. In more than a foot of river flow, water would be sucked into our engine and the oil would be emulsified. That would require a complete change of engine oil and we did not have storage for thirteen complete oil changes. We could seal the aperture to the engine perhaps and tow the car through each river. The distributor head on a Delage is at the base of the engine - not much more than a foot above the river bed! We could not practically waterproof it and use air feeder pipes and so we decided to spray it with silicone and include in our equipment a twelve-volt hair dryer to dry out our distributor. We were advised that we should have not less than eight inches of road clearance because of the many rough roads we would be tackling. Our lowest point was the front axle which has only seven and a half inches of road clearance. It was the best we could do.

Our spares and tools used up a high proportion of the back seat area which was the only [4] space we had for storage as the Delage has no boot. When we were told that, due to the absence of accommodation for some two hundred people in remote places, we would have to carry our own tent and sleeping bags, we were forced to dramatically reduce our planned personal luggage. Security was also to be a problem, particularly as the Delage is an open drop-head coupé. We have a canvas roof which can be raised but there are no side windows. We removed the back seat and formed the whole of the area behind the two front seats into a lockable area. In addition, we added a secure box immediately above the petrol tank.

The Classic Rally Association arranged for five RAC mechanics in one vehicle to act as sweepers at the rear of the ninety four entrants. It was made clear that whilst they would offer assistance, the responsibility for keeping the cars rolling towards Paris was that of the crew members. In the run up to leaving for Beijing, the Rally Association arranged two briefings at the famous Brooklands Circuit. On both occasions there was a feast of useful tips mixed with the odd comment which almost seemed designed to alarm entrants. An encouraging number of foreign competitors made the effort to attend. The final briefing gave an opportunity for cars to be scrutineered and approved. Waiting in the long queue to have my Delage scrutineered I was suddenly confronted by Jennifer Gillies offering a large tray of pastries. 'Would you like a hot croissant?' she asked with a delicious, slightly crooked smile. I inspected them more closely.

'I think they are pain au chocolat but yes, thank you.' I replied, returning her smile. She explained that the tray had been left on the back seat of her car (no 62) and that solar gain had warmed them to perfection. As she continued along the line of cars sustaining delighted fellow competitors, I reflected that if the Rally Association gave an award for the most popular entrant, she was the person likely to win hands down.

---

[4] Spares and tools listed in Appendix 3

After the initial restoration, we felt that the Delage needed to be thoroughly tested in preparation for the Peking to Paris Motor Challenge, so we entered it for the 1996 Monté Carlo Challenge in January/February of that year. Duncan and I also felt that we might benefit from the experience of competing in an International Rally. 1996 was the seventh successive time the Classic Rally Association had organised an annual Monté Carlo Challenge and the weather pattern included the worst snow conditions they had experienced. This caused the Association to offer competitors an alternative route via the French A8 - a virtual motorway. Duncan and I felt that we had entered the Challenge to motor through the French Alps and we did not want to be diverted. We made it to the finish and collected our finishers' awards, being eighth overall in the Vintage Section. However, just before the climb up to the Col de Turini, we broke the second gear. We thought the Delage would not make Monté Carlo but by charging up the Col in first gear and then whipping straight into third we made it to the top. Then we had to descend to Menton without second gear as a brake. We overcame this by fitting chains to all four tyres and creeping down through the snow and ice en route for Monté Carlo.

During our absence two men, David Whitehurst and Simon Gibson, had barely slept for the five nights of the Monté Carlo Challenge. Both are motor engineers and, though they operate separate businesses, they overlapped for the purpose of preparing and restoring our Delage. David re-built the engine and gearbox among many other tasks, whilst Simon restored electric's, brakes, shock absorbers, springs and steering. Their personal dedication was so great that, as we motored toward Monté Carlo, we knew that they were with us in spirit.

We returned to Derbyshire knowing a great deal more about our Delage and knowing that we had to carry out at least as much further restoration as we had already done if we were to tackle the Peking to Paris Motor Challenge with real confidence. All preparation and restoration was finally finished in early June 1997. We had little more than a month to test the car and build up our confidence in it before we set out at 08.00 hours on 11th July, 1997, to deliver the car to Debenham in Suffolk to be sealed in its container and shipped from Felixstowe. Before we set out for Debenham we photographed the car, which had been lovingly cleaned and polished. It was replete with Peking to Paris plates front and rear, its competition number, 10, and the names of the driver and co-driver. It also bore the name Team Spirit - the name of the two car team we had formed with Chris and Jan Dunkley (car 12) of Maidstone, Kent. We had met this delightful, married couple in the Monté Carlo Challenge when they competed in their beautiful 1935 Bentley 3½-litre open tourer. On both sides of the Delage bonnet were displayed the names of 'Norwich Union', the sole contributor of part sponsorship (the bulk of the cost being funded by me), 'Derbyshire First', a Derbyshire County Council initiative we chose to support, and our own Company, 'Norseman Holdings Limited'. The Delage is a famous, French vintage car but, in its colour of British Racing Green, it acknowledged the nationality of its crew. It looked resplendent and ready to hurl itself into the Challenge.

Insurance for the rally proved to be a considerable problem which was not finally solved until ten working days prior to flying to Beijing. I purchased an insurance policy to cover repatriation of the Delage, in the event of a break down in Asia which was irreparable locally. I also wished to have my normal fully comprehensive car insurance throughout the trip, but across Asia third party insurance had to be purchased at each border. As our sponsor, Norwich Union gave a special extension of my policy to make up the balance of my comprehensive insurance across Asia. For some inexplicable reason, however, it proved to be impossible to obtain repatriation cover for Turkey but that was in fact the only shortfall in our cover.

David Whitehurst and I drove the Delage to Suffolk, closely followed by my assistant driving my Range Rover as our return transport. How I later wished the roles of these two vehicles could have been reversed. Our arrival at the remote farm in Debenham, which was designated as the collection point, was an unusual experience. We drove down a long entrance drive past a half-restored, small Elizabethan farmhouse. The drive forked to the left past some rambling farm buildings in front of which a preoccupied and boiler-suited man fiddled with a tired tractor. Was this the place I was supposed to abandon my valuable vintage car? I was strongly reminded of the classic 'sting'!

The boiler-suited man was casual but amiable when I asked where the rally cars were being assembled and directed me to turn right at the end of the farm buildings. As I turned the corner I saw a large open barn with a Peking to Paris banner stretched over its double doors. A container truck stood in the yard with a single container holding another entrant's car, leaving just room for the Delage. Inside the barn was another boiler-suited man and a single seater racing car. He explained with an easy smile that the racing car had been there for some time as they were unable to identify the owner or the intended destination of the vehicle.

David Whitehurst was sad to part company with the car he had 'lived' with for over two years. I jokingly said that after all the problems we had to contend with I could easily kick it goodbye. Five minutes or so into our return journey I was relating how the unconventional arrangements for reception of our car had made me think how easily the whole thing could be a sting. In a moment of panic I asked: 'Did we even get a receipt?'.

'I have it,' my assistant said quietly. In fact the arrangements proved to be far removed from a sting, as the Delage later arrived safely and in good shape at the port of Tiangin to await my collection on 3rd September.

Chapter

2

I was intrigued by the pilot's frequent references to the Peking to Paris Challenge and the many competitors on board his British Airways flight from London to Beijing on Saturday, 30th August, 1997. I met the pilot, David Hall, briefly later in the following week and learnt that he is a vintage and classic car enthusiast who would dearly have loved to be rallying with us. It was my wife, Irene's, birthday on 31st August and, on that occasion, she lost one third of her birthday when we put our watches forward eight hours to Chinese time. Duncan and his wife, Sarah, were seated close behind us and we disembarked together at the beginning of our Asian adventure. Beijing airport was rather chaotic but we did manage to change some sterling for yuan. The Beijing Hotel was well short of five star but comfortable. We discovered later that this huge hotel had a recent extension called the Grand Hotel Beijing which was apparently five star. Both the buffet lunch and dinner were rather unappetising and with the onset of jetlag we ate lightly and siested but we did manage to celebrate Irene's birthday.

We slept later than we had intended on 1st September but then the four of us set off purposefully to see some of the sights. It was fine and pleasantly warm, although we were dismayed by the pall of smog overhanging the city. There were thousands of cyclists, pedestrians and rickshaw passengers breathing in black emissions from countless vehicles. Pedestrians were everywhere. For the first of many times I noticed that Chinese people habitually and without embarrassment stand much closer to each other than we do. Such proximity would be an invasion of privacy for most Westerners. We declined the persistent offers from taxi drivers and rickshaw pullers and walked less than a mile to Tiananmen Square. It was strange to gaze across this huge innocent looking square and to imagine the crushing of the student demonstration which had so recently caused such international outrage. There were many Orientals who seemed to be tourists but we saw hardly any Westerners.

With typical caution, Duncan and I felt that the four of us should stick close together as capitalist visitors in this Communist Police State. Duncan and Sarah had a slight disagreement as Sarah wanted to wander freely and soak up the enormous contrasts of the city and people. I noticed that one particular, local male of typically slight build, who had pushed his services as a guide of the Forbidden City, seemed to be watching our group from a short distance. He re-approached me and asked, 'You know Lady Di?'.

'Yes.'

'She dead.' It was not clear whether this was a question or a statement.

'No.'

'Yes, she dead. She killed in accident. Was she a good person?'

This is how we first heard about the tragic death of Diana, Princess of Wales. At first we thought it was some kind of cruel joke but later we heard the horrifying details of its reality.

All signs were in Chinese and it was with some difficulty we found the approach to the Forbidden City. There were endless traditional buildings with the trade mark, exotically curved pantile roofs. There seemed to be a different building in which the Emperor had considered each state issue which required his decision. Each was elaborately furnished with a throne and it seemed incomprehensible that they deemed it necessary to have a building for each type of decision. The concubines' quarters, built in 1420 A.D., were burnt down with much of the Forbidden City during an Anglo-French attack and were re-built in 1760 A.D. We smiled a lot but avoided speaking English! It seemed outrageous that one man and his immediate family required a whole city and thousands of wretched humans to serve their every need. Was it the slow growing seed of Communism?

After the disappointing dinner of our first night in Beijing, Duncan resolved to consult his 'Lonely Planet' brochure and find us a more interesting restaurant. By great persistence he managed to book a table, through our hotel reception, at 'Li Family Restaurant'. On arrival by taxi we had grave misgivings about the locality, the majority of which was shanty-type huts. The taxi driver parked and gestured to show Duncan the restaurant. Three of us were happy to let Duncan reconnoitre whilst we remained in the taxi, as we felt convinced the driver would want to return for his vehicle. I still felt edgy when they turned a corner and disappeared from view but they returned in a few minutes, Duncan pronounced it acceptable and the taxi left.

Li beamed as he greeted us at the door of his shanty. He led us through a small dingy room with two tables of four Chinese and six Europeans into a second, even smaller room with one table for two with Chinese diners and one vacant table for four, which was clearly meant for us. We sat nervously and looked around and though there was a clean white table cloth, the ceiling was lined with newspapers which had been whitewashed. The corners of the newspapers were having problems with adherence.

Duncan explained quietly that the presence of the Europeans in the first room had been the deciding factor before Li stepped forward gravely and offered a short, hand-written list of wines but which did include a Californian Chablis. I took that as an aperitif and there began the finest Chinese meal any of us had ever tasted. Li spoke elaborately enunciated English and soon introduced us to his niece who was the waitress and his first daughter who was the Chef.

There was no menu but Li gave us a careful description of each course as it was served. Our memorable meal comprised small portions in the following order:

Candied walnuts

Cabbage with mustard seed

Celery in home-made rice wine

Minced pork in lotus leaves, deep fried

Shredded pork fillet with pickled cucumber

Mung bean curd with chilli

Stir fry vegetables with chilli oil

Fresh prawns halved and deep fried in batter

Spiced beef

Sautéed potatoes in soya bean curd

Pork spare ribs with sweet and sour sauce

Steamed abalone with rape leaves

Deep fried scallops with rape leaves

Chicken sautéed in home made cooking rice wine

Fresh water mandarin fish with egg yoke, red and green peppers and
black mushrooms with ginger and mandarin sauce

Peking roast duck with hoi sin sauce

Watermelon

A second bottle of Chablis accompanied our best Chinese food ever.

Li progressively realised how appreciative we were and beamed as he expanded his delightful family's story. His grandfather had been chef to the Imperial Palace and had passed his culinary skills to his son who passed them to Li. During the Second World War Li had graduated in Chemistry ('Like Mrs. Thatcher', I remarked) at Peking University but his culinary hobby became his greatest skill. He was also very proud of his second daughter who, on the 35th Anniversary of the Federation of the Peoples' Republic of China in 1984, won a national competition to produce a dish to celebrate the event. The only interruption in our continuous pleasure from the arrival of the first bottle of Chablis was, mercifully on only one occasion, the jarring disturbance of a mobile telephone ringing on the adjoining table. They are just everywhere now. The bill was very reasonable but Li could only accept cash so it needed a whip-round to pay in yuan. His daughter ran for several blocks to hail a taxi and bring it back to the restaurant for us to return safely to the Beijing Hotel. We all slept well after an evening I shall never forget. Later we realised how fortunate we were to be able to book a table for the same evening at Li Li's when we heard that James Baker, former US Secretary of State was politely refused on another occasion because the restaurant had been booked months in advance.

The following day the four of us visited the Summer Palace - another small city with every form of staff to serve one family. When built, the Summer Palace with its majestic lake would have been deep in open country. Now it is in the outskirts of Beijing and its distant mountain views to the south-west are marred by the intervening and highly polluted industrial area. In the Palace grounds I walked the longest painted corridor in the world - according to the Guinness Book of Records. Studying paintings is one of my greatest pleasures but I found this corridor rather contrived. I would have preferred to see no paintings on the beams and less, but better proportioned, paintings on each side. Again, the Summer Palace was surrounded by numerous elaborate, enthroned, traditional buildings for every conceivable state and official event. It was another day which emphasised that, in China, reality and enchantment seem interchangeable.

The construction boom in Beijing greatly exceeds the flood of office buildings built during the 1980's, for example in Washington D.C. The new buildings in Beijing which find occupiers appear to be for state requirements or ex-patriot companies. I understand they are largely financed by the Chinese or investors from Hong Kong, Singapore, Korea and other Asian countries. There are striking looking new buildings many of which, for me, evidenced the style produced by American architects. Many have Asian variations such as sections of pagoda roof. It was suggested to me that some new buildings are vacant because of faulty structure. Examples given were a forty storey building where the lift only worked to the fourth floor because the structure was out of plumb; and another where the revolving restaurant does not work because concrete was poured into its mechanism. I understand there are apartment buildings where tenants pay US $8000 per month but the State can pay all living expenses so that take home pay, though low, is free for personal spending.

The Skitec Shopping Centre is housed in a rather drab building with a sixties look about it but inside it rivals Harrods for luxury of finishes and variety of goods. A new development adjoining the Beijing Hotel will provide eight hundred metres of new shopping on three levels. In my short stay I could not begin to equate the low salaries which are said to prevail with breakneck commercial expansion. Unemployment is rising but if the State decides to tackle over-staffing - thought to be three times the level of Western staffing - unemployment might bubble over.

Wednesday, 3rd September, was an exciting day - competitors were to journey by coach for about two and half hours to the Port of Tiangin to collect their cars. The road from Beijing to the port was mostly toll road so our cars were to have an easy first drive on Chinese soil. There were many clusters of single-storey barrack-like living quarters and man-made areas of water in the fields on both sides of the toll road - presumably so arranged for irrigation purposes. All of the cars had been required to sail with minimum fuel so there were long delays whilst everyone filled up with petrol and picked up mandatory Chinese licences, number plates and insurance. Competitors were agreeably surprised to find their cars parked at the port and looking much as they were when containerised for shipment. The only damage appeared to be one broken tail lamp, which was remarkable as the 'Feihe', transporting British cars, encountered a heavy storm in the South China Sea. Apparently the dockers were supplied with white gloves especially for handling our precious vehicles. We had our first taste of rigid convoy control by the police for the entire return journey. The police led us to the National Agricultural Exhibition Centre on the outskirts of Beijing which was to be our secure car park until the start of the rally.

Coopers & Lybrand invited me to take the Delage as one of ten cars to be displayed on the forecourt of the Beijing Hotel as a backcloth for a cocktail party they were holding that evening. Drivers and co-drivers were invited but not their wives. In addition we would have to travel to and from the party in police convoy, thus missing dinner. I declined. After dinner we went to an excellent party held at the newly opened Hard Rock Café courtesy of Prince Idris, driver of car No 9 - a 1932 Ford Model B Saloon, and his colleagues.

On Thursday morning we returned to the Exhibition Centre and busied ourselves arranging and re-arranging the packing of all spares and luggage. Duncan also removed the thermostat from the water cooling system as the car was running too hot in the warm weather - it was 85°-90° and humid. He also adjusted the brakes which had pulled to the left during our journey from the port. This was a day when entrants really began to mingle. The weather was warm and sunny and the atmosphere was one of cheerful excitement. In between packing and preparing the cars there was much wandering around the assembled cars, photography, humour and conversation.

Adam Hartley with Jonathan Turner in car 21 told us how four weeks before the start day, Jonathan had telephoned Adam to say that he had broken his right leg. Adam listened in stunned silence and thought of his two years of preparation but he knew Jonathan's humour well enough to recognise that this could be one of many attempts to 'send him up'. At that moment Adam determined not to be fazed, whether or not there truly was a broken leg. By the time they had finished discussing casually how it could be overcome Adam knew that Jonathan did have a break but that he was still continuing with the rally.

Dominic Kelly was determined to be in the rally even though the car owner he was going to crew for pulled out. He left his wife and children in England and flew to Beijing. He then put an appeal on the rally notice board saying he had all of his injections and offering to co-drive. His only offer was from an assertive, silver haired lady of around seventy years of age. He declined and flew home despondently. The silver haired lady had a story of her own. She demanded, only three months before the start, to be allowed to enter her three year old Rolls Royce but the Rally Association declined. Not taking 'no' for an answer she booked on British Airways to fly first class to Beijing. At the check in she said she wanted to take her car with her but was told this was not possible. 'What even for first class?' It was pointed out that this was a passenger aircraft but she was so insistent that she was allowed to take the car as excess baggage! In anticipation of driving ten thousand miles across Asia she had asked her dealer to give the car a normal service. In Beijing Phil Young explained to her that the car she had flown out as excess baggage was ineligible because it was only three years old and she was ineligible as no one was allowed to drive alone, for safety reasons. She fixed him with a direct stare. 'I've wasted a lot of money on this, young man.' The oldest person to actually compete was 72 year old Ray Carr, driving car 20, a 1939 Ford V-8 convertible.

After a sandwich lunch we rushed back to a Navigators' Meeting at 3pm. We both needed to be present as we were sharing navigation but nothing new came out of the meeting. Next we went by taxi to a reception for British competitors only at the British Embassy. We strolled in the very English garden and chatted to the staff about their role in this strong, Communist country. The Ambassador, Sir Leonard Appleyard, made a short speech and called for one minute's silence for Diana. Phil Young made a neat speech of thanks and then we all rushed back for a final briefing in the Banqueting Hall of our hotel. The acoustics were so appalling that most of us could not hear the questions raised or some of the answers so it was rather a fiasco. The day ended on a more relaxed note however, because we found the sumptuous bar of the Grand Hotel Beijing, where an excellent tenor and soprano serenaded us with arias. We asked for Harvey Wallbangers for all four of us and as the waitress seemed to understand our request we waited expectantly. When they arrived they tasted dreadful and I called the waitress and tried to explain in a friendly way the composition of a true Harvey Wallbanger. She returned shortly with four perfectly balanced drinks and there followed our most relaxed and civilised interlude in China since our arrival.

A very small percentage of Chinese people speak English and the reverse is more certainly true. How is it that two nation members of the human race can have so many similarities and yet have written and spoken language which is so dramatically different. It is true that our skin is a different colour and our eyes a different shape but our emotions produce fear, laughter and tears in similar ways. Yet their language cannot give characters for individual letters of names. Presumably Chinese is phonetic.

How fortunate we are that English, emanating from such a tiny country, has become the international language of the world. The beginning of its rise to supremacy was British colonialism followed by English speaking peoples' ascendancy in North America over French speaking people during the American Civil War. The French resent that such a narrowly balanced conflict in North America instigated the rise to supremacy of the English language instead of French. The English speaking United States then progressed to clinching victory in the 1st and 2nd World Wars and in the aftermath cemented the use of English as the first international language, world-wide.

Despite its fortunate accident of progress to first world language, English is eminently suitable. English speaking people have approximately half a million words to choose from giving a vast choice of single words which are brilliantly descriptive, albeit William Shakespeare, the greatest exponent of the English language ever, only used around twenty thousand words - about four per cent of the words available to him - to write all of his glorious works. Half a million words is far more than any other language - French offers only one hundred and fifty thousand. If one needed to rally the world against invasion by Martians, there is no more majestic language to use than English.

The day before the start of the rally we had to divide the tasks amongst the four of us as there were so many last minute preparations. Our wives did a great job of assembling the contents of our 'food bag'. This was a lightweight zipper bag gifted to us by the Rally Association and which we filled with fallback rations like tins of tuna, biscuits and jam. The girls even sourced a long handled Chinese spade which we strapped to our offside front wing.

Exhausted at the end of our day of preparations we set off for our last dinner together with our wives for six weeks. Duncan had heard of another good restaurant called the 'Old Duck' which specialised in Peking Duck. We had also considered - for half a second - the 'Sick Duck', so called because it is opposite a hospital, but the 'Old Duck' sounded healthier. The roads leading into Tiananmen Square were closed off that evening - we did not know whether the reason was sinister but it was certainly inconvenient. I think this was why our taxi driver missed his turn and dropped us in the wrong place. He gestured vaguely to the nearest building and foolishly we let him go. After thirty minutes of being directed backwards and forwards to no avail, I persuaded a young female shop assistant, who recognised the 'Old Duck' in the book we proffered, to walk outside with us and show us the way. All this, of course, with nil verbal exchange. I thought she would point the way from immediately outside but she gestured for us to follow her and she walked for so long that I had really given up hope of finding it when suddenly after at least five hundred metres we were standing in front of it. I was so pleased with the remarkable effort she had made, I wanted to reward her but she absolutely refused without letting her delightful smile slip. The four of us felt she was a wonderful envoy for the Republic of China and we hoped her long absence from work had caused no problem for her. We slept well on our last night in Beijing.

Chapter

3

It is said there is only one man-made structure on earth which is clearly visible from outer space and that is the Great Wall of China. That statement is, in fact, a fallacy scorned by astronauts but nevertheless, the Great Wall is a wondrous human achievement. Over a period of 2,000 years, 54,000 kilometres of defence wall was built. Strategically its use against invaders was of limited value so the logic of such huge, human endeavour is somewhat puzzling. If it was intended to keep out evil spirits, I believe its strategic value was even more dubious. Significant new wall and repair of the existing wall was carried out during the Ming Dynasty (1368 - 1644 A.D.) and its masonry hides the skeletons of many construction workers who died at their toil.

The Great Wall in the 20th century has acquired a car park for visitors some seventy five kilometres north-west of Beijing. It seemed a fitting place to arrange the Ceremonial Start for the rally, but first the Rally Association had to transport the one hundred and ninety competitors by coach from the Beijing Hotel to the National Agricultural Exhibition Centre, some five kilometres north-east of Tiananmen Square. On Friday, 5th September, the Exhibition Centre was the scene of last minute car preparation and packing, re-packing and even discarding luggage thought to be less than vital weight. The camaraderie really began to blossom with the excitement of knowing it was the very last day for preparation and wishing each other 'Bon Voyage'. Jill Dangerfield, co-driver to her husband Richard - driving car No 90, a 1965 Holden 3½-litre saloon - eyed my son and co-driver, Duncan, with motherly concern as she considered his prospects of travelling in our open-sided vintage Delage through the freezing Himalayas and burning deserts before finally muttering: 'You deserve a medal if you get that thing to Paris.' She shuddered at the thought of exchanging a seat in even their thirty-two year old saloon car for a narrow upright seat in a seventy-seven year old vehicle with a fold down canvas top but completely open sides.

The first car was due to start from the Exhibition Centre at 6.30am on Saturday, 6th September, and as car No 10 we were due to leave at 6.39am. We awoke to our alarm at 3.30am, breakfasted at 4.30am and left by coach for the Exhibition Centre at 5.30am.

This proved to be a presage of the pattern of morning departures. However, the times were rather academic as the police insisted on taking the entire entry of ninety four cars in convoy, led and followed by police cars. The prospect of my vintage car or the 1907 La France or even a 1974 Austin 1800 saloon running amok in Beijing and causing chaos seemed remote to me, but perhaps the Chinese Authorities did not wish these examples of capitalist opulence to be exposed to more than the minimum possible number of their citizens. It could be explained by a police desire to protect their people from wild Westerners used to driving on the wrong side of the road and hiding behind temporary Chinese number plates and insurance, supplied specifically for our crossing of China; I think it was more likely that it was another facet of a police state. This may seem a prejudicial reaction but it was not helped by the unsmiling countenances of countless policemen.

The spectators watching our departure from the Exhibition Centre were, by contrast, smiling, cheering and waving excitedly. It was rather disappointing to be convoyed the whole of the seventy-five kilometres to the official start from Badaling but we all went through the motions of having our time card stamped for the very first leg of our incredible journey. It was never intended to be a race but rather a timed rally. Except for six single rest days and two successive rest days in Kathmandu, on the remaining thirty five days of the rally each car was expected to leave on each morning at a specified time. A maximum of a half hour's lateness was allowed at each morning start and then normally a maximum of two hours lateness for time checks during and at the end of each day.

On the large surface car park at Badaling our cars were lined up in numerical order. We should have been leaving at one minute intervals from around 10.00am, but to our dismay we learned that the Chinese police would continue to convoy us for the remainder of that day. These were not the rally conditions which we or the Rally Association envisaged. Our wives and other supporters had followed us by coach to the Great Wall and they mingled with us and many local spectators whilst Chinese politicians and Phil Young, the Rally Association leader, made disregarded speeches. However, 6th September was the day of the funeral of Diana, Princess of Wales and everyone observed two minutes' silence out of respect for the Princess. My wife, Irene, and Duncan's wife, Sarah, hid their emotion at our impending departure behind their clicking cameras and then suddenly the convoy was moving away. A last tearful kiss and our wives had seen their husbands for the last time in forty three days. We had initially intended that Irene and Sarah might break up the forty three days by flying out to meet us when we had double rest days at Kathmandu, for example, but such short contact did not seem worthwhile relative to the amount of travel and so we settled for forty three days apart.

Just before we said goodbye my wife said: 'I want you to come safely back to me but don't forget you have our only son with you as well.' I was driving as we left Badaling and after our initial jubilation of finally beginning the challenge of crossing Asia, I began to reflect on what I had led my family into. My silence did not disturb Duncan. He was deep in thought too and in any case our relationship is such that neither animated conversation nor silence give discomfort to either of us.

I concluded that this rally was one of the least responsible arrangements I had ever organised for my family. It was definitely a reckless venture for the balanced and careful person I considered myself to be. Firstly, I had flown with my wife, my only son and daughter-in-law into the capital of a police state. 'What is so risky about that,' you may ask 'when tourists may now fly safely in and out of Beijing?' One difference which plagued my conscience was that we were part of a large visiting group flaunting its wealth via exotic motor cars in a totalitarian society. One of the first questions most local spectators asked was: 'What is the price of your car?'. Secondly, when all is going well the Chinese Authorities are dourly tolerant with visitors, but when crossed one would expect them to react in a repressive way to foreigners equal at least to the repression which they mete out to their compatriots. I had volunteered part of my family to join a rally led by Phil Young, a man renowned for his forthright opinions. Thirdly, I had abandoned my wife and daughter-in-law on a car park in Badaling. Certainly they were with a group of other supporters in exactly the same position - needing to coach back to Beijing and safely exit China via British Airways the following day. Irene and Sarah are both highly capable women but I knew that I would not feel comfortable until I could verify by telephone that they had safely returned to England.

The relief of hearing my wife's confirmation would be great but I would still have the responsibility of finishing the rally by reaching Paris with Duncan, totally safe and sound. I re-examined this thought. Duncan was thirty four years old, bigger and stronger than me and at least as mature. Also, I had invited him to join me on the rally and it was his decision to accept. Nevertheless, I knew that if my co-driver was a friend but not family and a problem arose, I would do my utmost to help and protect him but the pressure would be far greater with our only son as co-driver. The commitment was irreversible now and so I resolved to keep Duncan in focus until we returned to some semblance of civilisation which would probably be when we crossed the eastern border of Greece. As though our brains were programmed, Duncan and I concluded our reveries almost simultaneously and drifted back into conversation.

We drove through low mountains for a further one hundred and fifty kilometres, passing through a rally checkpoint at Huailai before reaching the first overnight stop at Zhangjiakou. Until one and a half years ago no Westerners had visited Zhangjiakou, except for an American couple who had lived there for six years teaching English. Naturally, the influx of over two hundred foreigners driving a variety of exotic cars drew most of the population to wonder at each arrival.

Lord Montagu of Beaulieu with his co-driver, Doug Hill, was driving car No 1, a 1915 Vauxhall Prince Henry four litre, but things did not go well for them on their first day. The radiator had been boiling over at intervals and then suddenly the cooling fan spun off and wrecked the radiator. The proud Vauxhall was destined for repatriation and Doug Hill was despatched home. Lord Montagu was not best pleased and needed to beg a lift in the 1967 Rolls Royce Phantom, car 42 driven by John Matheson and his co-driver Jeanne Eve. A lively American journalist, Chris McKenna, was relaying daily reports on the Internet and in describing Lord Montagu's reaction to the demise of his car referred to him as 'sour faced on a good day'. It was not a good day for Lord Montagu but he was later to show his persistence.

We caught occasional glimpses of the Great Wall on our first day's journey. Both of us regretted that the rally timetable had not permitted us to visit and actually walk part of the Great Wall. The lack of time to savour the sights and antiquities of Asia were an oft repeated regret. At least our wives had walked part of the Great Wall. The City Hotel in Zhangjiakou was a cruel jolt. We had expected hotels in the depths of China to be rudimentary or non-existent - on five nights we knew we had to camp as there was no accommodation which could approach sleeping over two hundred people - yet we were a mere few hours from the capital city and already the hotel conditions were appalling. The sheets appeared to be clean but the carpets were filthy. So much so that bare foot walking was unthinkable. The bathroom was disgusting. Not just because it had a hole-in-the-floor type of lavatory - we were expecting those - but there were holes in the tiled floor and the mesh cover over a floor drain had been thoughtfully removed to facilitate the ingress and egress of rats. The stench was like the worst public urinal you have ever encountered in Britain. I suggested to Duncan with savage humour that we should ensure that the bathroom door was firmly closed at night to avoid being eaten alive. We both tried to keep an open mind but we were dismayed that so soon on this long trip our mental markers for hardship and deprivation were inadequate. Welcome to Asia.

Chapter

4

I have always disliked being served food which defies identification, especially when it appears to have several components all of which are unidentifiable. Our first overnight stay produced such a meal and the slow decline in my weight began and continued until the eastern border of Iran. With 507 kilometres to drive the next day we needed to start at 6 am and so we picked our way into our beds at around 10pm, with some apprehension about the arduous prospects ahead. When Duncan's alarm awoke us at 4 am we both marvelled at the power of sleep to restore moral and energy. We consistently found that we needed to be awake two hours before our start time to prepare ourselves and our car as well as have breakfast. This was the start of our second day and there was a short panic looking for our time card before we remembered that we had left it overnight with the marshals. When we first started the car three out of four of the S.U. carburettors leaked. Duncan corrected this by tightening the banjo bolts to the float chambers.

We were disappointed to be again in a police convoy but it did have some compensations because we drove for the first hour in the dark and the Delage has very poor lights. We had installed two 12 volt batteries in parallel, one on each running board, and ancillary halogen spotlights but it was still like driving with flickering candles. Driving out of Zhangjiakou the convoy was very slow with many children and adults rushing out of their workshops to greet us. Hermann Layher in car 2, a 1907 La France Hooper, was the first competitor behind the police motorcycle outriders leading the convoy. Their pace did not suit Hermann and his car, sounding like an enraged traction engine, roared ahead of them on several occasions before the police screeched their rebuke. People were making their way to work and the traffic was heavy and varied, including hundreds of mules, most pulling small carts. Many of the carts were steered by a man who had a woman and children crammed in as passengers as well as a commercial load. Some of the mules with dark brown glossy coats stood out as superior handsome beasts. Parked in front of one workshop was a three tonne, second-hand, truck in fairly good condition superficially. It was priced at 62,800 yuan, equivalent to approximately 4,800 pounds sterling.

As the sun rose the ugliness of the industrial zone through which we were passing emerged. We could not see with great clarity because the pollution which pervades Beijing was present there too. There seemed to be almost a standard design for the jerry-built workshops which lined both sides of the road in pernicious strip development. The workshops looked like decayed teeth in the face of a beautiful mountain backdrop. Typically, they were single storey, forty feet wide, by twenty feet in depth with fully glazed frontages or half glazed with glazed tiled panels. This type of small building seemed to be used for every conceivable trade and even some element of living accommodation. Each workshop seemed to have its own pile of slacky coal which was clearly firing a most inefficient boiler pouring impenetrable, black smoke from a low chimney. This was our first glimpse of a level of pollution not seen in Britain since the Clean Air Act of 1970 began to take effect. The battered trucks serving the workshops competed with the chimneys in the black filth of their emissions. Rusty abandoned equipment lay everywhere. Shining out of this murk were the smiles of all the workers who rushed out to wave and cheer as we passed. The smiles were so broad, albeit with a very high proportion of decayed and missing teeth, that one competitor christened the crowds 'the dental parade'.

Motoring on into Inner Mongolia, south of the Daqing Shan mountain range and the infamous Gobi desert, towards the Yellow River, we were regularly passing through small towns and villages, all of which presented the same strip development of polluting workshops but now areas of strip coal mining and quarrying appeared more frequently. Between the towns and villages was heath land with many rifts; terraced, cultivated areas of sunflowers, maize and melons interspersed by endless waddies, which appear as dried up river beds formed by seasonal torrents. The faces of our spectators were progressively showing the characteristics of Mongolian features. Also, the landscape became more precipitous with lone, ancient watch towers. Several trains passed within view and blew celebratory horns for our benefit.

At this point, for the second time in two days, we lost our time card. The Rally Association had threatened competitors with expulsion or worse if we lost our time cards or route books. After only thirty six hours we had mislaid the time card twice so the chances of nursing our documents safely to Paris seemed remote. I felt responsible on this occasion as I was navigating when we suddenly found the time card was missing. I was convinced it had disappeared out of the open side but we stopped for a thorough search. Duncan found it had slipped well under my seat so we resolved not to leave the time card on the floor in future.

We drove on feeling relieved when I realised that I had left my sheepskin jacket over the battery box whilst searching for the time card. Later in the rally my jacket proved to be a lifesaver but even at that time I knew I could not afford to lose it. We had already begun to guard our sheepskins by wearing them whenever we left the car and taking them with us into our hotels. I felt rather foolish that within minutes I had lost a second piece of critical equipment. By now it would be lost somewhere on the heath and I stepped out of the car with a heavy heart to consider the options. To my relief I saw that my jacket had blown off the battery box on the running board, but had become tangled with the tool box on the back of the car.

Back in Derbyshire our engineers, David Whitehurst and Simon Gibson, who had given so much time and skill to preparing our car and instructing Duncan and myself about its maintenance, had already had their first sleepless night. In fact, at this point the Delage was running comfortably though other cars had run into serious problems. Francis & Casper Noz in car 18, a 1928 Ford Model A roadster, had already arranged for a trailer to repatriate their car as it did not make it to Beijing from the port. It must have been a crushing disappointment after two years of preparation not to even make the start. Car 62, a 1964 Volvo 122S Amazon, was also causing problems for its all-girl team, the Honourable Francesca Sternberg and Jennifer Gillies. Francesca is warm, gutsy and single-minded and has the distinction of being the youngest woman in the UK to gain an HGV (Heavy Goods Vehicle) Licence, whilst Jennifer has an inner strength and a hauntingly beautiful face. They rapidly caught the attention of the men on the rally and it gave me great pleasure to see them both on a daily basis. The suspension of the Volvo caused them more suspense throughout the trip than they had bargained for. They were disappointed with the outcome of the preparation work, particularly when a shock absorber broke on the first day.

The police had closed a new dual carriageway, giving the rally exclusive use for the day, and as we peacefully travelled its 145 kilometres length we had the beautiful mountain range of Daqing Shan on our right with distant glimpses of the Yellow River on our left. We entered Baotou, a town of some one and a half million souls, with the streets continuously lined with spectators on both sides. Refuelling proved to be an ongoing problem whether from a tanker or one pump in a fuel station. The logistics of feeding ninety odd hungry motor cars are protracted even at their most efficient. We were low on fuel and in order to avoid a long queue for petrol we pulled into a filling station well before the town centre. We were immediately surrounded by a milling, excited, gleeful throng of children and adults. No-one spoke English and we established the appropriate pump by a mixture of luck and deduction.

As Duncan drove away I continued writing travel notes in a green embossed notebook, presented to me for this purpose by Duncan prior to leaving England, and then fell asleep in mid sentence. Soon we passed the queue at the recommended filling station, where we could have had free petrol, and drove thankfully into the Tian Wai Tian Hotel for our second overnight stay. We had been warned that accommodation would deteriorate so we were agreeably surprised to find a good, Western standard of building with polite staff who were delighted to greet us.

Even though we had covered about 512 kilometres, being convoyed through two time checks - Jining and Tollgate, we were required to attend the first sitting of dinner at 6.30pm but we still managed a short siesta and shower before dinner. The section of good exclusive dual carriageway had certainly speeded our arrival and helped us to enjoy a civilised evening. On this occasion the food was more edible. The alarm woke us at 4am but we rose rested and cheerful. The police deemed it appropriate for us to proceed as a rally rather than in convoy so we were excited at the prospect of our first true rallying day. Our departure time was 6.05am and we were allowed four hours forty three minutes to reach our first time check at Xinbao. This was the time allowed for vintageants (cars built before 1950), whereas the younger, classic cars had a tighter schedule. Breakfast was a strange mixture so we concentrated on bread and took more bread wrapped in a paper napkin for lunch on the move, which became our habit. From thereon we had to navigate precisely as we were not being convoyed and we did remember that it was vital to zero our trip meter. In order to relate to the route book it was necessary to begin each day by returning the trip meter to zero and sometimes it called for us to zero at intermediate time checks during the day. The route book was in kilometres throughout and so we had replaced our mileometer with a kilometer. Duncan and I took more or less equal turns at driving and navigating and the navigator needed to be particularly alert in towns where a new instruction could be given after as little as one tenth of a kilometre. We also learned to live with our kilometer which read about 10% lower than the actual distance covered.

Chapter

5

We had 594 kilometres to cover on our third day and we knew that most of it would follow the wide Yellow River through the semi-desert of Inner Mongolia. After 60 kilometres the road dipped through a bad wadi which was the first of a series of paved and uneven waddies, bad bumps and poor road surfaces. We passed steelworks and many brickworks, all burning coal furiously and dirtily, interspersed with haymaking and crops of melons and water melons. Geese and seagulls were flighting regularly. The Delage was mobbed by spectators as we drove through Luihe with the crowd converging so that even at careful, slow progress the driver was in danger of running over feet on both sides. Our progress was slow enough to enable the crew to exchange 'hellos' with individual spectators. Some were keen to clap hands with the waving crew and Adam Hartley driving car 21, a 1929 Bentley 4½-litre VdP Le Mans, with Jonathan Turner, had his shoulder wrenched by a particularly enthusiastic fan. From then on we developed the technique of easing the waving hand behind the windscreen at the last moment to just avoid contact.

About 60 kilometres before Wuhai we were passing through semi-desert and in the distance beyond the Yellow River we could see the golden, rolling sand of the Gobi desert. The semi-desert was replaced by poor arable farming by the time we were 20 kilometres short of Wuhai and then as we approached the town the insistent waving of policemen convinced us that the time check had been moved to a site on the western outskirts. We were often surprised that we could drive for hours without seeing another competitor. It sometimes made us re-examine our navigation and we were pleased to recognise a gathering of familiar motor cars and that we had arrived at our second checkpoint with time to spare, having already arrived on time at our first checkpoint in Xinbao. In the first few days we and our 'Team Spirit' members, Chris & Jan Dunkley in car 12, a 1935 Bentley 3½-litre open tourer, tried to keep each other in sight but later we tended to rely on the rally four wheeled drive sweeper-up to cover the possibility of a complete breakdown.

Competitors are penalised for checking in too early as well as too late and, on this occasion, we had a little time to linger. Short terraces of poor, dilapidated, single storey shops and workshops lined the road with occasional gaps in the buildings leading to living accommodation at the rear, with haphazard enclosures for live stock. Between these enclosures appeared to be the only refuge for competitors needing to relieve themselves. Two pool tables stood on the forecourt, one was in constant use by successive foursomes of young males. Other shopkeepers and locals sat languidly on battered stools and the other pool table, which was damaged beyond use. A young woman casually leaned against a wall, breast feeding her baby. Duncan opted to drink Coke and guard the car whilst I wandered over to the group around the damaged pool table and asked for a Coke. Inside the nearest shop was a tired refrigerator, but it produced a 'safe' drink. I believe I drank more Coke on the whole rally than I had drunk in the previous thirty years. An old man gestured for me to take a stool opposite him and even with no common language it became obvious that he was the local cobbler. He sat in warm sunshine surrounded by hammer, last and nails waiting for customers. I gestured an offer to play pool but he declined and I offered him an extra strong mint. He took it and I saw from the interest around me that I had other takers. They all smiled revealing a golden opportunity for expanding dentistry in Asia and a youngish woman disappeared into her shop and returned to give me a water-melon. It was a satisfying exchange of contact and as the rally progressed I often wished for more time to pause and make one-to-one contact with local people. At my suggestion Duncan and I swapped roles so that he could meet them also.

We had covered over 400 kilometres but we still had a further 194 kilometres to travel on the final leg of the day. Every school and even army camps that we passed turned out in force to cheer us on. Similarly all industrial and commercial staff seemed to erupt from their buildings as we passed. Every man, woman and child in all villages seemed to leave their homes to wave and cheer. Already we estimated that we had seen hundreds of thousands of spectators and concluded that there must have been some kind of Government directive to the population. We realised that since leaving Beijing, where apart from ancient, traditional Chinese buildings, there were new buildings with interesting combinations of Western and Oriental styles, the standard of architectural design across Asia was abysmal. The standards of construction always looked poor and their elevations were devoid of beauty. In Yinchuan we re-fuelled about two kilometres before reaching the Yinchuan International Hotel on time at 6.28pm. Once again we were agreeably surprised at the standard of our hotel, particularly after the Zhangjiakou Hotel, which was possibly the worst hotel I had ever encountered. The Rally Association had arranged for competitors to have dinner at an outside venue, a State-run restaurant, but we stayed for a passable meal at our hotel. Later we heard from many competitors that they wished that they had stayed with us.

We had another early start time on our fourth day - 6.05am - and so we fumbled about in the dark when the Delage developed its first fault. Our car normally started very readily and it did on this occasion but then it very soon stalled. We juggled under the bonnet with the fuses and re-started the car but soon it stalled again. Rushing now to make our start time, we changed the fuse and this time she kept going. We had three hours fifty five minutes to make our scheduled time at Zhongwei and we began with a lengthy drive through semi-desert. It never ceased to amaze us as the trip progressed, what an incredibly high proportion of Asia is desert, semi-desert or at least arid. At 53 kilometres on our trip we reached Xaoba where the Muslim architecture in the market place was exotic compared with the drab buildings since Beijing. Again, an army camp and schools turned out en-masse to see us. Since leaving Baotou we had been traversing China in a south-westerly direction in the long journey towards Tibet and around 20 kilometres after checking-in on time at Zhongwei, we entered an area of rugged loess - an Asian type of soft sandstone - hills with many recesses and caves cut into the stone. Some were still inhabited by monks and shepherds, and sheep and cattle roamed the area. A much higher proportion of people in Muslim dress were in evidence. The landscape was very arid and barren, yet beautiful.

Twenty kilometres east of Jingtai, crops re-appeared and soon we heard blasting from a quarry we were passing. After negotiating a minor accident between agitated locals we pulled into a filling station and were immediately mobbed by a crowd of children and teenagers. Later we reached the summit of a Pass at 8060 feet and after two hundred and seventy five kilometres we joined an expressway where we were waved through the toll, as happened on subsequent occasions, presumably because they had been paid or cleared by the Rally Association. We also passed through a cutting in the loess which was raked back very steeply, perhaps at 50°. We arrived at the excellent Fei Tian Hotel in Lanzhou, having checked in on time at 5.11pm. I was still picking at food over dinner but it was a relaxed enjoyable meal with Duncan, our team mates, Chris & Jan Dunkley and Richard & Jill Dangerfield (car 90). We went to bed early savouring the thought of our first rest day, albeit we had many minor Delage ailments to correct including fusing side lights. It was very civilised waking up on Wednesday, the fifth day of the rally, with no checking out time to make. I savoured a full English breakfast, remembered to take my anti-malaria Larium pill and joined Duncan for a maintenance session on the car. There were many small items of maintenance and I was impressed that Duncan appeared to have cured the fusing problem before we made it for a late lunch. In the morning session we also discovered that a bolt securing the radiator had sheared so that the radiator was moving so freely it was in danger of fouling the fan. The consequences of the fan meeting the radiator did not bear thinking about.

After re-packing and a siesta we met the same lunchtime group for dinner and Richard persuaded us to drink wine from the supply he carried in his boot - a pleasant way of helping him to reduce the overall weight of his car. We retired early in anticipation of another 4am wake-up call. I habitually paid my hotel bill for extras immediately after breakfast and so on Thursday morning, just as we were about to leave at 6.10am, I was surprised to be accosted by a messenger claiming we had an unpaid hotel bill of 6 yuan equating to about .40p. He refused to take money and tried to pressurise me to go back into the hotel and resolve it. I refused but the encounter did nothing for my humour and stumbling along in the pitch dark I almost collided with a cyclist without lights and later a pedestrian who crossed without looking. Not a good start.

We overtook a number of competing cars which were parked on the side of the road but were displaying the recommended 'OK' sign to indicate they did not need help.

When we saw the police car which was leading us in convoy out of the city we realised that for the first - and only - time we were the leading vehicle. This meant that when the police car pulled aside on the outskirts of the city we continued for another 16 kilometres as lead car, meaning that we had to be extra sure of our navigation. We arrived early for our intermediate time check at the Hotel Xining and when Chris & Jan Dunkley joined us later they complained that I had driven too fast. On the second leg of the day we passed high walled compounds with guard towers, which looked very much like prison camps. The scenery softened later with oxen hauling ploughs, the harvesting of grain, a horse pulling a grindstone in a circle over spread corn and hay piled on the flat roofs of small houses. Duncan was startled when he noticed that our off-side headlamp was behaving in a less than sober manner. One of the bolts securing it had sheared in surrender to the lumpy and potholed roads. We took it off and stowed it rather than risk it falling off completely. We soon needed to stop again. This time our spare wheel, mounted on the nearside and with an extra tyre and innertube attached to it, also joined in the insobriety. We put up our 'OK' sign again as we inspected the damage. A bolt and the spare wheel mounting had sheared so that the nearside front mudwing and running board were taking the weight of the spare wheel. It was fortunate that we spotted the damage before it increased and we used a ratcheted strap to hold it temporarily in position.

We had passed through an area of terraced fields, which were almost alpine in configuration and were being harvested, before we settled onto a straight, level road with dry, mud brick walls - the Asian equivalent of Derbyshire dry stone walls - set back some twenty meters on both sides of the road. I had the beginning of a stomach bug after breakfast that morning and realised that I was monitoring the distance between occasional gaps in the wall as a possible emergency escape to find some element of privacy behind the wall. I soon realised that the monitoring was becoming dangerously like roulette as there was no consistency in the distance between the gaps and so I decided to stop at the next gap. It was a good decision - and timely. A female competitor had stopped at the previous gap but fortunately they were far enough apart for modesty to survive. The truck we passed shortly afterwards was rather less sanitary - it had many shallow tiered decks packed with live chickens. A lone, mournful yak on the roadside must have at least valued his relative freedom. It rained most of the afternoon which was not encouraging as we were to pitch our own tent that evening for the first time on the rally. The Delage's water temperature was again causing us some concern. It had dropped to 12° which does not make for efficient combustion and wear. We liked it to be 140°-150°. Yet we were reluctant to refit the thermostat with our increasing penetration into the Himalayas. We checked in at Koko Nor thirty-three minutes late and incurred our first rally penalty. Fortunately the rain stopped long enough for us to pitch our tent and dodging the rain reminded us of when I took Duncan as a child camping near Windermere in the Lake District. The Rally Association had organised a team of Gurkhas to travel this part of the journey with us to cater for our camp dinners and breakfasts. I found dinner on that first night of camping much more edible than some of the hotels, which was fortunate as I was still suffering from a stomach bug.

The 1907 La France, driven by Hermann Layher with his co-driver John Dick, was undoubtedly an even more uncomfortable car to drive than the Delage, especially in bad weather. The crew of the La France were perched up above the engine level with not even a windscreen to provide an element of shelter. We heard that, earlier that day, the co-driver had given up the battle against wind and icy rain and hitched a ride on a passing bus. Hermann staunchly drove on alone but eventually became so cold he was forced to pull just off the road and seek shelter in a solitary yurt - a small rawhide tent, in which huddled a Tibetan family. Later, one of the rally support crew arrived on the scene and stopped to investigate the deserted La France. He discovered Hermann in the yurt, delirious and clearly suffering from hypothermia. Hermann was hospitalised and developed pneumonia. He was eventually returned to his home where he slowly recovered, as we continued across Asia. The La France was out of the rally and was joined in retirement from the event by car 11, a 1919 Marmon, with a damaged drive shaft and by car 6, a 1930 Stutz, with electrical problems. The number of cars continuing had dropped to ninety.

Duncan and I found the width of the Delage very constricted, particularly when we were wearing our thick, sheepskin flying jackets, when the navigator needed to sit slightly at an angle so that his right shoulder did not impede the driver's steering and gear changing. Our two man tent was also constricted particularly as we needed to sleep in most of our clothes with that vital piece of equipment, the flying jacket, over the top. We did stay warm through our sixth overnight stay and although we awoke on half a dozen occasions due to the hardness of the ground - we should have had inflatable beds - we managed to get back to sleep quickly. The Sherpas who prepared the camp site for the rally group also had problems with the frozen ground which hampered digging the latrines. The sparse habitation of the countryside surrounding our camp site was a considerable contrast with the heavy population in the towns and cities we had passed through. Our seventh morning started well with a good breakfast and everyone ready to go from 7am. Several other cars stuck in the mud and needed a tow and those cars departing later became involved in the aftermath of a bus accident. Twenty one locals were injured and some of our competitors and paramedics helped to free trapped passengers.

I had a wonderful drive rising through many hairpin bends and reaching a sandy plain at the top. At one point I had to brake sharply, having been 'cut up' by Don Saunders in car 15, a 1932 Packard 903 convertible, as he pulled in sharply after overtaking me. Duncan was surprised but I said at the time: 'Worse things happen at sea.' Don later offered his 'abject apology', confirming the characteristics we had already observed - the consistency of his courtesy as well as his humour. About fifteen kilometres before Dulan we crossed a huge fertile plateau ringed by distant mountains and again featuring the roadside mudbrick walls. From time to time we passed Tibetan monks walking towards Lhasa who regularly threw themselves into prostrate positions, as required by their religion. We had often seen the tents of single shepherds or road maintenance workers but here we saw a small village of tents presumably for agricultural workers as well as herdsmen. It was easy to see why many Asian (African too) people have more respiratory problems than those in the most urban areas of

Britain. Open fires were burning in the tents with smoke emitting from blackened holes in the roof. People sat around them for warmth and cooking, resigned to the damage to their eyes and lungs. The hawks wheeling above must have pitied the smoked humans below. After six and a half hours we checked in on time at Qinghai and in the afternoon we had another five hours or more of motoring to reach our overnight stay at Golmud. We travelled over two hundred kilometres through the most arid, featureless landscape of desert and semi-desert. I called the endless grey shale, virtually without vegetation, a 'gravel car park', probably the largest car park in the world as it stretched almost flat to the horizon on both sides of road 109, which lay like an arrow through the centre at a bearing of 300°. This desert was uniformly the dark colour of shale rather than golden-red sand. It was relieved only by a very occasional thorn bush.

Chapter

6

All competitors were tired when they reached Golmud - some much more than others. We arrived on time at that time check and were pleased and relieved to reach the Hotel Golmud. Our pleasure was short lived, however, because one minute later we saw our room. The bathroom was a similar horror to the first night in Zhangjiakou, the bedroom carpet was again filthy but this time the sheets were unpressed and decidedly suspect. Once again, we slept in our own sleeping bags on their unopened beds. The water system was prone to ceasing without warning and we kept our use of it to a minimum.

We were just leaving our room feeling rather disgruntled about its poor state and making for the dining room to see what new horrors awaited us when Richard Dangerfield intercepted me excitedly: 'Do you know that someone has run into your car?'

'No. Who?'

'I was standing at my window looking over the car park and I saw the driver clearly in a fury, back out fast and accidentally reverse into the side of your car. He didn't get out he just drove off.' I went out to inspect the damage and found the front off-side mudguard was badly dented but it did not affect the mobility of the Delage in any way. I shrugged it off as other things in our apology for an hotel were of greater concern, and went in for dinner. I did wonder whether the driver would apologise when he had cooled down.

We slept remarkably well on, rather than in, our beds and rose at a relatively civilised time of 6am for an 8.09am start on our eighth morning. I reminded Duncan to take his Larium but he was ahead of me - his day for Larium was Saturday, mine was Wednesday. We were pleased to leave Golmud and start the 'Roof of the World' section. Initially we had a lumpy road running through more 'gravel car park' type of desert and I wondered whether the millions of acres of arid land we were driving through had been caused by the meteorite storm which damaged the East and Middle East, supposedly, around 2350 BC. Soon we began a long steep climb with a beautiful river in a deep, sheer cutting on our right and a wolf silhouetted dramatically on a ridge. This we felt was serious rallying and our spirits rose. Serenity was disturbed when a bolt sheared on the radiator stay, for the second time, after I saw a serious rut too late and drove through it too fast. A simple problem to rectify but symptomatic of the effect of driving the Delage continuously over very uneven roads which were simply shaking our car to pieces. It is hard to describe the feeling of anxiety, approaching anger, one feels when driving continuously over a road which is wantonly destroying one's beloved and valuable car. The only way to relieve the destruction was to drive at a hopelessly inadequate speed for our timetable. Flighting pigeons and an eagle were indifferent to the ruinous road and to the yaks blinking in light snow.

We were down to second gear as we laboured up the long, steep road to Kunlun Pass but we made it to the top where, from a height of 16,000 feet, we surveyed the awe-inspiring vista of moorland, some of it snow-covered and with many peaks. As one rises to a higher altitude the quantity of oxygen progressively diminishes and, in an internal combustion engine, the injection of petrol therefore needs to progressively decrease to maintain the balance of the mixture of petrol and oxygen, but we made the decision only to change the carburettor jets to give a weaker mixture if, and when, the Delage gave up. We were rather pleased with the way her engine and carburration had coped with the altitude as our S.U. carburettors seemed to have allowed the Delage to rise to higher altitudes rather better than the Volvo Amazon's or David Bull's 1965 Rover 3 litre P5 coupé, which were missing at low revs. We realised that any stop for repair work was likely to make us late and we were four minutes late checking in at Glacier Plateau on the Kunlun Pass. We had an allowance of four hours and six minutes to do the remaining 204 kilometres to our eighth overnight stay, camping at Tuotuoheyan. After sixty kilometres we encountered semi-desert again although there were cattle, including yaks, searching for grazing. After a hundred kilometres it was snowing lightly again which did not bode well for our second night under canvas. An eagle with bold brown and cream feathers took off close to our front wheels as we swept by and disturbed its roadside rest. Perhaps because of our gradual reduction of speed to minimise car destruction, we arrived sixty seven minutes late for our over-night check in on a camp site at Tuotuoheyan, having covered 439 kilometres. Duncan and I were unperturbed about the rally penalties we would incur by being late. We were within the permitted lateness of two hours and therefore, we were still eligible for gold medals at that point. In any case, we had already agreed that we did not care about winning medals, never mind the rally. Our only objective was to reach the finish in Paris on October 18th with both of us and our car safe and intact. It was of the utmost importance for us to be rally finishers in our Delage, but we felt that was challenge enough without feeling driven to win.

Fortunately the snow had stopped when we erected our tent but it was cold and dark. Duncan had prepared an inspection lamp on a long lead which clipped to our car battery and provided the one glimmer of civilisation. At least we could see the gear we needed to take out and put in our lockable compartment - it was a godsend. I felt quite cheerful as we made our way to the group of tents where supper would be served. After the food produced by the Gurkha team on our first night of camping at Koko Nor, I felt confident that I would be able to eat a normal quantity of wholesome food and I did have some catching up to do. I also bought a bottle of red wine, called 'Great Wall', to share with Duncan, from a tent designated as the bar. In order to feed over two hundred people a series of 'dining' tents were erected. I went slightly ahead of Duncan and sat next to Peter Cordrey who was seated against the canvas back of the tent. Peter and Gordon Phillips were the drivers of car 56, a 1961 Rover 100 P4. I noticed that Peter was offering nothing in the conversation with fellow competitors around the table. In fact he looked thoroughly miserable and dejected. I leaned towards him and said: 'What do you do for fun?' Peter contemplated this question in silence for a few moments and then roared with laughter. Many times later in the rally he looked more positive than I felt.

I derive a great deal of pleasure from smoking one cigar a day - a Cuban Montecristo No 2. My wife and my children certainly do not encourage me to smoke even one and doctors always advise against any smoking. My family accuse me of becoming philosophical when I smoke but I do not subscribe to Woodrow Wyatt's theory that 'smoking is good for your health'. I had smoked one each evening since arriving in China but at Tuotuoheyan I did not. It was my small gesture in acknowledgement of the warnings about Acute Mountain Sickness which doctors suggested would affect, perhaps, seven percent of our group. I was keen to avoid needing to resort to those pathetically small canisters of oxygen in our medial kit. Duncan and I had considered and rejected the idea of taking Diamox, a drug to reduce the incidence of AMS. Some people swore by it, others said it had no effect but, worst of all, some developed side effects which replicated the symptoms of AMS! Full circle, which is why we rejected taking the drug. In any case, whether or not you have taken the drug, if you develop AMS the only cure is to move to a lower altitude as rapidly as possible. The only way to go down fast from the 'Roof of the World' section of the Himalayas would be to go down by helicopter, but helicopters do not thrive at that height so you are left with the unsatisfactory resort of driving back the way you came or forward to Kathmandu. Neither are likely to be quick enough. Surprisingly, AMS is more likely to affect younger people and so I was keeping an extra watch over Duncan.

I used part of my flying jacket to cushion my head and a small inflatable cushion under my hip when I slept that night and enjoyed a much more refreshing sleep than our first rally night under canvas. It was Sunday, 14th September - our ninth morning of the rally - and out of the sleeping bag it was very cold. Our problems were about to begin in earnest. As usual, we started the Delage before breakfast in case there was a problem and we needed more time to attend to the car. It started promptly even though the temperature was low enough to cause us to thoroughly de-ice the windscreen and lights. Chris and Jan Dunkley parked and camped next to us and so we witnessed Chris's unsuccessful efforts to start his Bentley. Chris was calm and deliberate in his efforts to coax the Bentley but Jan was understandably increasingly agitated. She is a brave and able woman but would any woman be relaxed about being stranded in a frozen field in a remote part of China with the prospect of all other competitors and back-up team leaving them alone with the uncommunicative Chinese police?

Our Delage was due to check out at 8.08am and as eight o'clock approached Chris and Jan repeatedly urged us to leave them as the back-up team, in the four wheel drive

Vauxhall Frontier, kept trying unsuccessfully to start them after each attempt at adjustment. Having witnessed Chris's unsuccessful attempts to start, the back-up team had moved in with enthusiasm to help. Duncan and I retreated to distance ourselves from their efforts to avoid distracting them and confusing the issue as to who should be working on the Bentley. Two members of the back-up team, Tim Riley, known as Jingers, and Trevor Shaw had taken over and become very absorbed in the challenge. I thought how my wife, Irene, would feel if she were my co-driver in Chris's silent Bentley and the Dunkley's were raring to go in my Delage with its engine throbbing consistently. I knew that Irene would be comforted by my presence but even more comforted if the Dunkley's waited to see us safely out of that field. I looked at Jan pacing out a huge rectangle around the Bentley as a calming exercise whilst the fruitless efforts to start the Bentley continued. I knew I did not want to leave them. I spoke quietly to Duncan: 'If we wait here until the Bentley starts and miss our own check out time we could find that we are more than two hours late at the next time check, in which case we will have lost our chance of winning a gold medal. What do you want to do?' He replied without hesitation:

'Stay. They're members of our two car team and they have a problem. In any case, our strategy is just to finish, not to win medals'. Also, we both agreed that if we did not lose our gold medal at the next check in we could eventually lose it by having to rebuild our own car en route. So it was decided that we would stay. We refused all entreaties to leave and I think Chris and Jan were somewhat comforted by our presence. After increasing pressure from Mike Summerfield, the Clerk of the Course, Jingers and Trevor finally reluctantly admitted defeat and towed the car off the field to the road where Jan had negotiated to have the Bentley trucked to Lhasa. Minutes before this Duncan came to me and said quietly: 'We have a serious problem of our own.' He took me to the rear of our Delage and I saw with horror, petrol running like a slow tap from the bottom of our fuel tank. We had waited almost two hours thinking we had a healthy car only to find we were likely to be immobilised. We discussed the options. We could not replace or repair the tank before Lhasa and the leak was too great to be staunched by the traditional temporary methods of chewing gum or opal fruits. There was a filling station about five kilometres east - back - and we needed a full tank to reach the petrol tanker which was the next available fuel 433 kilometres away at our overnight camping stop at Nagqu Camp. We retraced our route and filled the tank with the only petrol available - low quality 70 octane. They did not notice our slow running tap until we were driving away. Their consolation was that they had overcharged us by 50%.

When Duncan and I finally waved goodbye to Chris and Jan they were driving their car off a mound of earth to which the truck had backed up. A crude method, but the only method as the trucks had no ramp or lifting gear. Another entrant, John Matheson, in car 42, a 1967 Rolls Royce Phantom V, found to his cost that this method of being driven onto the back of a truck could cause more damage than that which disabled his car in the first place. This crude loading method was something of an indignity for his Rolls, which started life as Queen Elizabeth II's official car on State visits to Australia. The Delage was at last underway, although we knew that we no longer had any chance of winning a gold medal. We saw many birds and beasts as we bumped along, forever anxious about our leaking tank. We saw yak, a herd of highland cattle and a large flock of sheep. Eagles and owls flew above us and a vole shot across the road in front of us. We had reinstated the off-side headlamp on our rest day, but shortly after we crossed an ancient wooden bridge we noticed it was about to fall off again. We secured it temporarily with a bungee cord as we were close to our checkpoint. Finally, we reached the highest point at which a rally control point has ever been located, Tanggulashaukou, at almost 17,000 feet the highest road in the world, the 'Roof of the World'. Having left that morning almost two hours after our scheduled start time we checked in at the 'Roof of the World' two hours and eight minutes late. Later that evening we went through the formality of asking the Clerk of the Course for dispensation because we had waited for our team mates. He quite correctly pointed out that it was our choice and therefore, he could not give any dispensation. After taking in the magnificent views and congratulating each other on having made it thus far, Duncan busied himself by taking off our loose headlamp. We did not want to see this beautiful, though useless, specimen bounce off the road as a replacement, if you could find one, would cost at least £500. I opened a can of tuna, spilling the oil on the battery box and leaving a stain which still remains. David & Pat Dalrymple, driving Car 26, a 1949 Cadillac Series 62 coupé, experienced their first car problem of the rally at the Roof of the World, when their regulator gave up. At the outset of the rally they believed that they had one of the most unsuitable cars but, in the event, it gave less trouble than the majority of other entries and was certainly one of the most comfortable cars. Adam Hartley's 4½-litre Bentley, car 21, had a different problem. With thin air and low octane petrol his engine was so puny on steep slopes that Adam and his co-driver needed to run alongside the car using the hand throttle.

Duncan was struggling to remove a nut from a rusted bolt which secured the headlamp. Eventually, after considerable effort, he freed it and staggered around the car and placed it on top of the rear secure compartment. Belatedly I remembered that in the high altitude of the Himalayas one should avoid any exertion and I turned and focused on Duncan. He looked pale and rather unsteady: 'Dad, I'm not feeling too well.' I bundled him into the passenger seat, picked up the tools and flung them alongside the removed headlamp, clambered into the driving seat and drove off purposefully. You cannot speed when you are descending from the highest pass in the world, but I did not hang about. Fortunately the road dropped quickly towards Amdo at the junction of the main highway to Western Tibet and Duncan soon felt better. Although I was very concerned that we had five more days driving through the Himalayas before we reached Kathmandu, we never rose quite as high as Tanggulashanqu again and mercifully, neither of us had any further hint of altitude sickness.

Delage leaving official start at the Great Wall

Car number 2, perhaps the most intrepid competitor

Yellow River

Gobi Desert

The Delage covered every inch of the route under its own power.

Cave dwellings in Eastern China.

Enthusiastic young spectators

Camels in central Asia

Cabbages in central Asia

Unlicensed 'people carrier'

River in setting of arid beauty

Roof of the world

Falling apart at Xigaze

Mount Everest

Desolate Tibetan road

Rough Tibetan road

Landslide-prone road between Choksham and Zhangmu, on the Chinese/Nepalese border

River bed just before Chinese border

More wild road leading to border

Colourful locals in Zhangmu

Birds-eye view of road from Choksham to border

Spectator sport

Chapter

7

On our second leg to Nagqu we saw many hawks wheeling above pasture land with herds of sheep, yaks and wild ponies. For a spell we were embroiled with a convoy of twenty identical army trucks and it took us a long time to overtake them one by one. We were just too slow to overtake a line of them. We also passed a nature reserve which seemed incongruous in this wilderness. We completed the second leg of 235 kilometres within our allotted time of five hours and fourteen minutes and so incurred no further penalties. Our fuel tank was practically dry when we checked in at Nagqu and there was a huge queue of vehicles to the petrol tanker which was the only supply of fuel. We were both exhausted and so we decided to eat supper first and think about fuel afterwards. As though to punish us for this indulgence, we found that the tanker had run dry and it was 'hoped' that it would return the following morning. The tanker did arrive the next morning though it taxed us still further by arriving late. We were not penalised for the slightly late start however, but were scheduled to reach the intermediate time check at Damxung by twelve noon.

We did not make twelve noon. The front nearside wing lost bolts and stays - it was hanging on but literally by a wing and a prayer. Rather than rely on prayer we rigged up a temporary strap and checked in one hour sixteen minutes late. However, in between anxiety about bits dropping off and the leaking tank we were impressed by the scenery. In Duncan's words, we travelled along a single road across a huge green plain with a backcloth of foothills, snow covered mountain peaks, cotton wool clouds and patches of clear blue sky. 'Workmen' often appeared to be children, including a herdsman I would have put at twelve years old and a labourer of perhaps ten years. As we entered Damxung we saw a woman pounding her washing with a wooden dolly like the one my grandmother used. Fifty kilometres into the final leg to Lhasa we found a filling station and topped up our leaking tank with fifty litres of petrol. Soon after the Delage began to perform rather badly and was missing at low revs. We wondered if there was water in the top-up of petrol, but we motored on hoping it would not deteriorate further. We passed a parked police car and were surprised and pleased to see him wave cheerfully. After 100 kilometres we drove through a fertile valley where wheat was being harvested and wagtails strutted on both sides of the road. Just before Lhasa we passed a large granite quarry and motored on the last ten kilometres to reach the Lhasa Holiday Inn on time and with considerable relief.

Car 43, John Van der Laan's 1958 Citroën 2CV, had a rather more precarious arrival in Lhasa. Its suspension was broken and the co-driver, Willem Graal needed to stand in the boot to raise the wings off the front wheels. Fortunately, they repaired the suspension overnight, avoiding the necessity for Willem to maintain his balancing act for hundreds of kilometres. Other problems were experienced by Ivar Moe and Peng Yew Wong. Ivar's car 84, a 1969 Morgan Plus 8, was overheating and ingeniously he cut down a plastic bucket and used it as an extra cooling scoop for his radiator. Peng Yew Wong's car 37, a 1954 MGA sports, collided with a bicycle and was fortunate that the only damage was to vehicles, including his front wing and headlamp.

We had considerable debate during the journey to Lhasa where we were due to enjoy our second rest day. We knew that we would have to work all through the 'rest day', even though we were staying in the religious and economic heart of Tibet, if we were to make our rally start time the following day. The most important issue was what to do about our leaking tank. We agreed there was no chance of replacing our tank in Lhasa with a new one, with only one free day. I suggested we could take four 20 litre jerry cans of petrol, fill the tank to just below the leak and use the jerry cans to top up between filling stations. We had now established that our badly designed petrol tank had developed a leak through a split in the tube which passed through the middle of the tank to provide partial support. A seamed welded tube had been used instead of an extruded one. The seam had split and petrol spilled from both open ends of the tube. I suggested we cork the two ends but Duncan thought this would not work. We discussed it with Jingers who thought it would be feasible to replace the tank in Kathmandu. We compromised by agreeing to buy jerry cans in Lhasa, to limp to Kathmandu and then replace the tank.

The next morning, Tuesday, 16th September, our first task was to find jerry cans. We set out in a taxi with a driver who spoke only Chinese. The one aid we had was a piece of paper with the words 'jerry cans' written in Chinese. We toured round and round in the taxi hoping that the driver would take us to a jerry can vendor or we might see the kind of shop that could sell them. In the process we saw the Potala Palace, home to the Dalai Lama from the seventeenth century until his flight into exile in 1959. We also saw Jokhang Temple and much of the teeming commercial centre of Lhasa - perhaps more than we might have seen as 'tourists' for the day. Eventually we returned to a street where I had seen two shops which could stock jerry cans and the driver parked and motioned us to walk while he waited. We had seen no other Westerners anywhere near that street but we set out to go sign shopping. Both shops had them but only old ones in plastic not metal. We had no other choices so we bartered with both and bought four from one delighted shopkeeper and we also bought a large length of rope to secure our mud wing and anything else that might fall off before we reached Kathmandu. We did not have time to organise welding as well as complete our leak contingencies. After ditching some gear, moving all of the tools out of the rear box and strapping the four full jerry cans standing in the tool box, we just made it for dinner. We were sorry to be leaving such a comfortable hotel without having the chance to savour it but at least we had a civilised start time the following morning - 9.22am.

On the morning of Wednesday, 17th September, the twelfth day of our rally, I privately rated our chance of reaching Paris in the Delage at no more than about 30%, a sorry fall from the high hopes in Beijing. I thought the chance of reaching Kathmandu was no higher but if we did make that psychological hurdle, we would have two rest days to repair the car and re-assess our chances. The Rally Association had planned two separate routes from Lhasa to Xigaze, one for vintageants and another more difficult route for classic cars. In the event, under pressure from the Chinese police, they cancelled the more difficult route and sent all cars on the less difficult road. We would have had the option to take the more difficult route and, with the state of the Delage, I was quite pleased to be relieved of that decision. We left on time but had to proceed at a more cautious pace to avoid jolting the fragile plastic jerry cans. We passed first through semi-desert and then beautiful mountains with a deep gorge, terraced strips of crops and a fast flowing river. In between many areas of white water, the colour of the river was the same alpine green that typifies rivers swelled by melting snow in the European Alps. We checked in on time at 10.56am by Lhasa Bridge and 11.41am at Khamba La, two intermediate time checks. From Khamba La, at a height of 15,600 feet, we had a majestic view of many peaks to the south and the beautiful turquoise lake of Yamdrok Tsho. After descending from Khamba La we followed the shore of Yamdrok Tsho and then passed an impressive hanging glacier.

We heard the sound of our near-side running board support shearing and stopped quickly to inspect the damage. Both running boards were rather critical as each supported a box containing a twelve volt battery and tools. The bracket needed to be welded and so our temporary repair was yet more roping up. The length of rope we had bought in Lhasa was something of an afterthought but it was already proving to be an invaluable addition to our kit. The slow pace on the steep incline meant that the car was discharging too frequently. We were already concerned about the strength of our batteries and so we needed to use second and third gear to keep the dynamo charging. Once we had crossed the great Yarlung Zangbo river we were driving due west and we knew that across the remainder of Tibet we would be travelling on dirt or gravel roads, often in poor condition.

We arrived at the time check in Gyangze seventy six minutes late and realised that we no longer had our camera. It was a bitter disappointment because we had taken ten photographs of the beautiful landscape both approaching and leaving Lhasa. Fortunately our team-mates, Chris & Jan, had also felt compelled to photograph the scenery we had found to be the most beautiful on the trip to date and they comforted us with promises of copies. We thought back over the day remembering some of the ragged children looking like Fagin's urchins who had surrounded our car whenever we stopped and guessed that our camera had been stolen. We loaded up my reserve camera and vowed to re-double our efforts not to leave it in view whenever we stopped. I took to carrying it around my neck but Duncan would not succumb to this tourist trade mark.

45

When we reached Xigaze - sometimes called Shigatse - for our twelfth overnight stay, we were again late by forty four minutes. We had only covered 272 kilometres in the whole day but it had been a tough route particularly with an ailing car. We were relieved that we had not been allowed to choose a stiffer route. By this time we had reversed roles with Francesca and Jennifer who had a tottering time with their fault ridden Volvo up to Lhasa. Now they were much more relaxed and we were nursing the Delage. Nevertheless, Duncan and I managed to siesta before dinner.

Chapter

8

Our start time the following morning, Thursday, 18th September, was a civilised 9.22am. We only had a total of 309 kilometres to do in the day but we knew that, once again, it would be a tough route. We were not optimistic about our prospects as we reviewed our leaking tank, lashed running board, battery and amperage problem. We wondered which we would lose first, battery or amperage We acknowledged that we were hanging on by our finger tips. We limped out of Xigaze using first and second gear to maximise charging the battery. As our anxiety plateaued, we noticed a very slight improvement in the design of dwellings, some of which had parapets above moulded wooden windows with projecting stone lintels above. We passed many road workers and, after about 100 kilometres, we saw a monastery perched on a hill above road marker 5000 indicating that we were 5000 kilometres east of Beijing by road. I swerved to avoid a mule and ran headlong through a vicious pothole uttering furious expletives and pleased that at least my wife was not listening as co-driver. The road works caused muddy off road diversions but at least charging was not a problem as we crawled through in low gear, trying to ignore the fact that we were running late again. The many warnings about ground clearance had sections like that in mind.

We passed through Tsuo La Pass at 4,500 metres and began a steep descent, eventually reaching a time check at Lhaze thirty one minutes late. I expect you find the similarity of some of the Tibetan names as confusing as we did. We ate a hasty buffet lunch - what a luxury - zeroed our trip meter and set off on the next leg along a very bumpy road in a steep sided valley. We stopped briefly for Duncan to buy local crystal from a running child vendor for the princely sum of two yuan. We wound our way up through bleak moorland to the Gyatso pass which, at 16,900 feet, is about sixty two feet higher than the Everest Base Camp, the highest point on our road between Lhasa and Kathmandu and the watershed between Tibet and India.

The Rally Association brought the final time check location forward to Gyatso Pass and, as the distance was reduced to thirty four kilometres, they reduced the time allowance for vintageants to forty one minutes. It was nothing like enough to cover that

47

testing route. We checked in seventy-seven minutes late and I remarked tersely that I doubted I could have done it in forty one minutes driving my new Range Rover let alone a vintage Delage. We still had another 119 kilometres to drive before reaching the camp site and the road conditions did not improve. Oblivious of our tortuous efforts to slow down the disintegration of the Delage, a vole scurried across in front of us. We saw large mixed herds of mules, cows and goats and a huge flock of pigeons erupted into flight.

A fuel tanker ground past us about half an hour before we saw it parked on the side of the road filling up another entrants car - a mobile fuel station. This was an opportunity to fill up rather than waiting for the inevitable queue on the camp site. The driver was reluctant to fill up our jerry cans but eventually we persuaded him to fill them all as well as half filling our fuel tank and, as it was the rally tanker, we did not even have to pay. Our joy and amusement were short-lived - the Delage would not re-start. We rolled back on to the roadside, tested the batteries and found them both completely flat. Luckily the sweeper vehicle soon appeared and gave us a jump start. It was a case of 'Don't even think about stalling' and of course we had to keep the ammeter charging positively but at least the scenery was stunning with green mountains topped by small fringes of rock. The dirty windscreen did not help but we dared not stop as we wanted to reach the place, about 50 kilometres further west, where there was the possibility of viewing the highest mountain in the world, Everest. Duncan lifted the front of our canvas roof as I drove and wiped away the worst of the accumulation on the windscreen.

I became increasingly doubtful of our ability to reach the likely viewing point for Everest in time as there was some cloud cover and daylight began to fade. I was incensed by the prospect of the timing not working and the likelihood of passing Everest without seeing it, as it was one of the principal attractions of making the trip for me. I began to push the Delage as much as I thought it could stand. It was dusk when we finally saw several competing cars stationary on a bridge whilst the crews were all focusing their cameras in the same direction. The view of mighty Everest was heart-stopping. Its peak was entirely bathed in the setting sun whilst its base was screened by the unlit contrast of a range in the foreground. It was so beautiful that I thought the timing had worked well by bringing us to the viewing point just as the sun was setting. It was one of the most uplifting and triumphant moments of the entire rally. We photographed and soaked in the awe-inspiring spectacle of Everest before returning to our car. We had left the engine running hoping she would not peter out and Duncan drove the last six kilometres to the Everest or Xeger camp site. We arrived in darkness but were pleased to see a paler version, from a slightly different angle, of that world famous mountain. We handed in our handbook to the marshall as soon as we arrived to confirm the arrival of car 10. That evening was the first time in the rally since the start, when every competing car had been penalised.

The unfortunate Mick Flick, the Mercedes heir in car 74, had a bad tooth pulled out with pliers from his tool kit. By contrast, we ate and slept fairly well though, by morning, clouds obscured Everest and our expressions were overcast too when the

Delage refused to start. After breakfast we arranged our second jump start and drove hopefully off the site. After less than 10 kilometres a mule ran directly at the Delage causing me to brake hard and swerve wildly. Fortunately she did not stall and I continued along a road with washboard corrugations. This is one of the most testing surfaces for any car and one of the most trying for its driver as it is impossible to avoid vibrations and at frequent intervals they build up to a demonic pitch, which can only be eased by slowing to a crawl. Some drivers believe washboards should be attacked and that higher speeds will rise above the periods of demonic pitch. In my experience, if one tries that attack method in a vintage car, it is heading for 'melt-down' disintegration. We checked in at Munboche on time and continued over the high plain of Lalung La before climbing in light sleet to Lalung La summit, at 5050 metres, for another time check. The road, which was repeatedly subject to repair works, descended steeply with many sharp bends until we joined the valley of the Pö Chu River which was to be our companion to beyond the Nepalese border. The road was cut into a steep rock face with a near vertical drop to the river far below. On our left we saw the Cave of Milarepa, a seventh century teacher renowned for his poems.

On this latter section of road, the first serious accident occurred. The driver of car 70, a 1965 Mercedes Benz 220A, and one of the few cars occupied by three people - Peter Janssen, Gunter Klarholz and Wolfgang Meier, sounded his horn as he overtook a stationary bus. A Tibetan road-worker stepped from behind the bus to cross the road just as car 70 reached the front of the bus. There was no opportunity to prevent a collision and the worker was bowled over and landed in a heap with a broken leg and concussion. The rally doctor arrived shortly after in a back-up vehicle and tended the patient in a nearby building. The local policeman who appeared on the scene was not unfriendly but insisted on the driver waiting to be interviewed by a senior policeman who had some distance to travel. The driver had to wait for an anxious five hours before the senior man arrived but then within three minutes he had interviewed and released him. The doctor was harangued by some of the local people who wanted him to stay and continue treating the patient but eventually he was bustled into a rally car and whisked away. Someone suggested that had it have been a Chinese worker rather than a Tibetan worker, there would have been more serious repercussions. Even relative to China, Tibet still has the air of a poor, occupied country and it seemed hard to comprehend that in just over one month, the 21st October, 1997, it would be the fiftieth anniversary of the Chinese occupation of Tibet. After the accident the Rally Association declined to operate time checks, other than to check for safe passage, until after Kathmandu.

The valley had widened and we again saw oxen pulling ploughs. When we reached Nyalam village we had a mere 20 kilometres to reach our hotel but unfortunately, the route book caused some confusion at that point and competitors were seen to be disappearing in opposite directions. Car 12, the Delage and two other competitors carried on through the village rather than drive straight on just before the village. The disconcerting thing about our route was that the route book referred to a view of Nyalam village some 8 kilometres after we had driven through it and yet the topography was such that it was clear we were never going to see Nyalam again unless we retraced the last 8 kilometres. At this point Chris Dunkley decided that he had made the wrong decision and that we should all return to Nyalam. The narrow and precipitous road made an about turn extremely difficult and, in any case, I was adamant that we should carry on as the route book directed us 'into Nyalam', whereas the route taken by other drivers meant going straight on just before Nyalam. Thankfully I was right and we finally arrived at the Choksam Hotel for our fourteenth overnight stay. Another earlier case of a competitor being lost was rather more amusing. An Italian co-driver, wishing to have his route book stamped at a time control, asked a policemen where he could get a stamp and was taken to a post office in the nearest village!

Choksam Hotel was built around seven years earlier, it closed after a year and then was re-opened that day for one night specifically to accommodate the rally. There was no lighting, no water, the public areas were uncarpeted with broken slabs and gaping holes over the central service duct in corridors. This meant that 'residents' were required to edge along one side of the corridor in the dark to avoid falling down the holes. Everyone found some form of personal lighting, a torch, a miner's headlamp or a candle. The bathrooms were dark pits of horror with broken evil smelling unwashed fittings and the bedrooms had large cracked and broken windows. The bedroom floors could have been carpeted although it was impossible to be sure from their irregular surface. The bedclothes were rejected by us at a glance. A few competitors had found a small meadow opposite and pitched their tents for the night and, comparatively, it looked idyllic. It occurred to me that, in Britain, Choksam Hotel would be closed instantly for any one of a hundred reasons. I told Duncan that I would rather camp but he said that he felt he would have more sleep in his sleeping bag if it was at least supported by one of those awful beds. So we agreed to stay in an hotel which made the first night's hotel look like the Dorchester.

I was unhappy about the security of my open car parked in the road and I had been told that, if I could negotiate the rocky outcrop which masqueraded as a steep drive, I could park the Delage in the yard behind the hotel where it was visible through our broken window. Nigel Challis in car 96, a 1955 Land Rover Series 1, helped me by jump starting the Delage and promising to drive up and do the same the next morning. I gave the Delage a short sharp lesson in rock climbing and parked it within sight of my room. It was difficult to dredge much humour out of Choksam but when I asked Sarah Catt for my room key our ace, unflappable accommodation organiser, apologised that there were no keys but gave a room number. I strolled into that room and startled a dejected looking male competitor sitting on the bed and, as we both claimed that it was our room, his voice thinned and rose in agitation. I suppressed a smile, offered to go and resolve it and returned to Sarah. I always found her attractive and womanly as well as consistently cheerful and helpful in spite of being deprived of sleep more than most competitors. It had already occurred to me that if one needed to be stern with Sarah it would not be enjoyable and I simply said: 'I'm afraid the room you gave me is already occupied.' Her face was a picture of shock and confusion but she quickly recovered, checked her records and gave me another. It was unoccupied and I quickly moved our bags in before any more squatters moved in.

The atmosphere in the public room, dimly lit by oil lamps and supplemented by torches as people walked in and out, was surprisingly good. There was no dancing or singing but most people seemed resolute about rising above the squalor. The Gurkha cooks at least maintained their standards of good edible food whilst we endured the Choksam Hotel. Again, we slept remarkably well and when I rose next morning, on Saturday, 20th September, and looked across the fast flowing Pö Chu River in its steep ravine, I recognised the stark contrast of the Choksam Hotel as a supreme example of an appalling creation by man being placed in a location of outstanding natural beauty.

I established that the Delage would not start, had breakfast and recruited Nigel Challis again to provide a jump start. It was only 24 kilometres to the frontier town of Zhangmu but it proved to be the slowest, most concentrated section of bad roads in the rally. We were led away in a police convoy at a snail's pace and soon the winding road, which was cut into the very steep side of the ravine, became an obstacle course. There is a bridle path near my home in Derbyshire which I would hesitate to negotiate in my Range Rover. Yet the road to Zhangmu was worse and I was attempting it in a vintage long wheel-based car. There were landslides, waterfalls to drive over and through, rockfalls, streams and beds of ugly rocks and thick mud as well as the usual hairpins. No part of it was surfaced. At one point, just after Kjeld Jessen driving car 8, a 1929 4½-litre Bentley open tourer, drove under an overhanging cliff, he heard a violent crash behind him. A large rock had been dislodged by the vibrations of the Bentley and was blocking the road. It had to be moved by competitors who followed before any other vehicle could squeeze by. We had an additional problem - we had to keep our speed low because of the appalling surface but our revs high to keep the battery charged. The cars were all moving in a slow column down this horrendous 'road', which was mostly only one vehicle's width, so once again it was a case of 'Don't think about stalling'. To maintain this precarious balance I was literally healing and toeing the brake and accelerator whilst working the clutch.

Several other cars broke steering or springs or suspension during that first 24 kilometres before we limped into Zhangmu. Much about the village and its people looked perhaps more medieval than Dickensian. The locals were as astonished to see ninety exotic cars and their dramatically different occupants as we were relieved to have reached their village with its close proximity to Friendship Bridge and the Nepalese frontier. The Bridge was specially opened for the rally for the first time in twenty years but first we inched our way in a queue of cars through Zhangmu with the locals wide, appraising eyes, following our every move. Every fifty metres or so a currency dealer would pressurise us and try to begin a haggling negotiation. Duncan was driving and I strolled in the narrow streets attempting contact with locals who were not currency touts and talking to other competitors. In one exchange with Peter Noble of car 61, a 1955 Bentley Continental Mulliner, he remarked sagely: 'When you are rallying, anxiety is always with you.' In view of Peter's considerable rally experience, his comment gave me some comfort that our own anxiety was fairly normal and balanced.

51

We received a wonderfully enthusiastic welcome as we crossed Friendship Bridge from the local people including the Nepal Red Cross. They gave us necklaces of marigolds - a sign of honour and welcome, and we congratulated each other and our friends and fellow competitors on making it across the whole of China. Soon we resumed our journey, limped our way through many road works from the border passing the United Nations Post at Launindauda and jubilantly arrived 108 kilometres from the border at the time check in the Kathmandu Convention Centre. We spurned waiting for the rally bus, jumped into a taxi and checked into the excellent, five star Yak and Yeti Hotel. Duncan and I drank a bottle of Dom Perignon with dinner to celebrate our survival thus far. Etienne Veen, driver of car 7, a 1927 Mercedes 630K sports, was not so ready to celebrate. His magneto had failed so that the Mercedes had the indignity of being trucked into Kathmandu. His co-driver, Robert Dean, was even more concerned as he had sold his house and all that he owned to enable him to take part in the rally.

A group of workshops at the rear of the Convention Centre had been allocated for rally repairs and on the morning of Sunday, 21st September, ten Nepalese mechanics were assembled for the purpose of trying to help to reinstate as many broken and deficient rally cars as possible during the two 'rest' days of Sunday and Monday, 21st and 22nd September. Sambhu was the acknowledged leader of the mechanics. He was fiftyish and lean with long, grey hair, an unhurried walk and a cool but ready smile as he squeezed the humour out of the desperate pleas from owners of ravaged cars. He knew he was the man of the moment, not because of the work to be done as most competitors were able and willing to do it for themselves, but because he could source and deliver the diverse parts and components which were urgently needed by them. It was difficult to obtain Sambhu's focused attention amidst this desperate, clamorous group of fellow-competitors and even more difficult to retain it for long enough to activate the obtaining of parts and in some cases the carrying out of work by mechanics. Nevertheless, Sambhu was admirably cool and remarkably successful in the requests he satisfied.

We worked non-stop throughout Sunday and Monday organising the welding of broken brackets and refitting the head lamp, spare wheel and running board. The Nepalese welding equipment had no electric plug and was operated by sticking two bare wires into the wall socket. Our lunch was snatched at the Conference Centre food court so that our only sightseeing was from taxis as we collected spares and travelled to and from our hotel. We had both batteries tested and found that one had failed completely and the other was suspect. I left the suspect one with Sambhu and fitted two new twelve volt batteries which we hoped would work well and consistently for the remainder of the journey to Paris. The cost of replacing them was not significant in the overall scheme but the anxiety about discharging with poor batteries was very much to be avoided.

Sambhu felt that the leaking petrol tank could be repaired by gently hammering whittled, wooden plugs into each end of the split supporting tubes. I was rather gratified that my simplistic idea of corking both ends was supported by an engineer. He also thought that to source or make up a suitable replacement tank and fit it would take too much time, particularly with the time he and his team were allocating to the multiple problems of other competitors. Duncan remained sceptical but we watched a mechanic saw two small pieces from a hammer handle, whittle them to plug shapes and gently hammer them in. We then refilled the tank to the top and waited fingers crossed for the plugs to work. We knew that petrol would soak into the wooden plugs but we hoped that it would only produce an occasional drip. Within minutes the nearside dripped every few seconds and the offside every second. Duncan quite rightly felt it was not good enough and decided to make two new plugs by sawing two pieces from the end of our wooden dip stick, which was originally formed from a broom handle. The mistake the mechanic had made was using bits of an oval hammer handle whereas Duncan would be whittling plugs from perfectly round bits of our dip stick. In order to remove the first plugs we first needed to siphon the petrol from the tank to below the leak. Siphoning from a tank with a rubber tube into jerry cans requires sucking on the end of the tube to induce the flow which should then continue. Technically one should be able to stop sucking just before one's mouth fills with petrol but I can testify that a little practice is needed to achieve the correct timing. Unselfishly I insisted that I sucked the tube rather than Duncan and although I achieved the flow of petrol I had to gargle away the foul taste of petrol with Coke. I could still taste it after breakfast the following morning. I asked Duncan to keep an eye on the jerry can whilst whittling the plugs and switch over to another when it was full. The Nepalese mechanics watched with some amusement as Duncan whittled away at replacement plugs and I later learned that the flow of petrol had stopped on the changeover and so Duncan also had to gargle with Coke.

Whilst the jerry cans were filling I wandered over to the adjoining car 54, a 1952 Mercedes Benz 300B, driven by Werner Esch and his delightful daughter Sylvia Esch. Werner worked alongside us on his car throughout the two rest days and Sylvia called in regularly to talk to her father, easing our toil with her warm smile. I had first noticed Werner adjusting his brakes early on the first 'rest' day and whether lying with feet sticking out from the car or hauling himself from under his beautiful Mercedes, he looked a seriously contented man. Our many conversations during the two 'rest' days informed me that he hailed from Luxembourg where he was a major Opel dealer - Opel being the European version of Vauxhall in Britain. Werner insisted on preparing his own car rather than relying on the many mechanics on his staff and so he was rather enjoying a busman's holiday in carrying out maintenance during the rally. His Mercedes was so well prepared that problems arose much less frequently than other rally cars and he was ever-ready to help other competitors with their problems or breakdowns. He would have been my choice had there been an award for the man most ready and able to help other competitors. He took a fatherly interest in Duncan's efforts to overcome the disintegration of the Delage and frequently offered nuts and bolts from his wide selection, as well as the loan of tools.

When Duncan had finished the second set of wooden plugs he extracted the first set, tapped in the second set and we refilled the tank. The new plugs also became soaked with petrol but there was only an acceptably infrequent drip from each side. Duncan was gratified and the Nepalese mechanics admired his improved repair. It was almost sunset on the second day when we concluded our repairs. All the ropes, straps and bungee cords were taken off and re-stowed with spares and so we felt that we had virtually restored the Delage to its rally start condition. We just made it to a reception at the British Embassy and for dinner at the Yak & Yeti Hotel before retiring for a comfortable night's sleep till 6am on Tuesday, 23rd September.

Chapter

9

We checked out promptly at 8.07am and we both felt sad to be leaving Kathmandu, having spent so little time exploring the city. Duncan was also feeling nauseous and said very little as I negotiated heavy and varied traffic on the western route out of the city, but both of us were startled to see a muzzled bear being taken for a walk on a lead. Leaving Kathmandu behind there was much terracing of the hills and in the rear ground the twin peaks of Manaslu and Himal Chuli. The road improved after Naubise and followed the Trisuli River, suitable and used for white-water rafting. When we reached Malekhu cheering school children lined the streets, although we were left in no doubt they were organised rather than spontaneous. In Mugling our route notes warned us not to accept invitations from ladies. Rather a sweeping direction, I thought. Our route along the valley of a tributary of the Ganges, the Narayani, showed signs of flood damage so that, though the road surface was much better than we had been used to, one could never afford to drive in a relaxed way - complete focus had to be maintained. A monkey sitting on the side of the road caught our attention but the driver needed to switch back to the road quickly to avoid being surprised by water splashes of varying depths.

We were delayed as we drove through Narayangadh, a busy town with streets thronged with pedestrians, trishaws and buses and so reached our time check twenty eight minutes late. We noticed that more roofs were thatched and we passed through a wooded area not dissimilar to the New Forest in England, before arriving at the time check in Butwal - this time on time. We checked in eleven minutes late at Bhalu Bang and then on the last leg of our 500 kilometres day we passed through beautiful scenery on the edge of the Royal Chitwan National Park before reaching our eighteenth over-night stay - camping at the Sapridi Trading Compound at Kohalpur. We filled up with petrol just before the camp and were somewhat dismayed as we were directed into what seemed more like a commercial trading estate. We found Nepal softer and greener than Tibet and after skirting the National Park it was disappointing to spend our last night camping on a site well removed from that rural idyll.

Despite the dreary location the organisers of the site had made more of an effort to accommodate us than had been made on any other camp site. As well as the usual latrines, they had provided canvas enclosed washing areas where buckets of water and bars of soap provided crude but effective ablutions. They had also erected a whole series of neon lights which made individual torches unnecessary, though each neon was a magnet for flies and insects, the great billowing clouds of which were all too visible. A single large tented area was used for supper, which on this one camping occasion was not supplied by our trusty Gurkhas, but with ample electric lighting and open-fronted canvas we were eaten by insects slightly faster than we could eat our food. Despite the efforts of the organisers it was by far the most uncomfortable camp site. The only relief from the plague of flies was when I smoked a Montecristo No2. Friends sat closer than usual to squeeze into my no-fly zone. For a short time there really were no flies on Ashby! Our two man tent in complete darkness also provided some respite from the weight of circling insects and so we retired early and sleep shut out the enemy.

Our nineteenth morning saw the end of rally camping and for some reason we were decidedly less organised in preparing for our check out at 7.07am, but I did remember to take my Larium. (To maximise one's defence against Malaria it is necessary to take one tablet on the same day each week of an Asian visit, as well as for two weeks before leaving home and for four weeks after leaving Asia.) Shortly after leaving the camp site we saw a peacock on the roadside and then cruised down the Mahendra Highway on a fairly good asphalt surface, to our first checkpoint on Kanali Bridge, the construction of which was donated to Nepal by the Japanese Government. We arrived on time after two hours of driving and set off immediately on another section of just over two hours to the Indian border. The road now became very rough as it skirted the largest area of wilderness in the Terai, the Royal Bardia National Park, home of Bengal Tigers. This was the section where we knew there were at least thirteen river crossings and Phil Young was at pains to put his competitors on red alert, with his dark warnings of rivers to be crossed flowing quickly at depths of one metre; that may not sound very deep but it is enough to sweep most cars down river. Our route book contained a special tip sheet for river crossings: - take the fan belt off - you do not need a fan in water; spray the fuse box and distributor with WD40 just before entering water; drive slowly; keep the revs up but speed down; do not stall - as water would be sucked up the exhaust pipe into the engine perhaps bending valves or con-rods; do not dither; let water in by opening the doors rather than floating off; and finally do not pay too much to locals for pushing your car otherwise you lift the price for people behind you. In fact, the water was lower than the dire warnings had suggested and I drove through all of the fords at a slow but steady speed with revs maintained and a quick surge of speed just before the far bank so that the Delage managed every one without faltering. Those competitors who did stall were usually trying to cross too quickly and paid the penalty of having to be towed or pushed out. A lone stork was disdainful of the unusual activity in its stretch of river.

We arrived at the small dusty town of Mahendranagar, the last Nepalese town before the Indian frontier, without having untied our tow rope from around the front number plate. It was a special kinetic rope which was used by taking up a stranded vehicle rather faster than usual so that the spring on the rope could pluck the stranded car out of deep mud. I was very happy not to have needed it. For a few days prior to arriving at the Indian border many rumours were exchanged between competitors about the likelihood of aggravation and delay in entering India for the rally cars. The rally seemed to breed rumours. Some were created by the desire of one competitor to send up another, but each time it was repeated and believed it gave a boost to the perpetrator. Others were stimulated by wishful thinking or a desire to extract a reaction which might lead to confirmation of the rumour. In my experience rally rumour-mongering was second only to rumour manufacturing in the armed services. The most frequently repeated story was that the Rally Association had paid a fee of fifteen thousand pounds sterling to support the extra staff needed to facilitate a smooth and speedy passage through Indian customs but, at the eleventh hour, they were asked to pay a further ten thousand pounds sterling, they refused and the mooted response was a work-to-rule by the Indian officials.

We were never able to confirm whether or not it was deliberate but in customs and passport control there was much laborious registration and re-copying of detailed information about each of the ninety rally cars. Even the most jocular complaint about the tedious progress was stamped upon fiercely by officials. In contrast, free crates of Coca-Cola were distributed to the queues of tired, dusty, hot competitors. Perhaps we were seen as the innocent victims of a foundered negotiation. We checked in at the border on time but it took five hours to pass through the frontier and so it was 16.33 when we at last checked out. We were allowed three hours for the final leg of the day to Nainital. In fact it took four hours and most of it was driven in darkness.

We passed through the frontier gate with a sigh of relief, along a dam wall and near the town of Tanakpur. On both sides of the road we saw goats, cows and monkeys wandering freely, though a horse had its front legs tied together to prevent it from straying. After about 30 kilometres we saw herons near to another large dam and a sign of colonial influence as we passed locals absorbed in a game of cricket. The vegetation was more lush than Nepal but provided sharp contrast with the dry, dusty roads and villages. Presumably the healthier crops were a product of irrigation and water pumps. We drove through the busy small towns of Sitarganj and Kichha with more and more industry and the accompanying pollution as we approached Haldwani just over 100 kilometres beyond the border. The town of Haldwani was crawling with every shape and size of vehicle intermingled with darting unseeing pedestrians. Finding the correct way through the heaving turmoil in the dark was far more luck than judgement.

Nainital is a mountain resort of over 6,000 feet with some winter skiing but it also has a beautiful lake with promenades alongside. Before independence, the British found it a fashionable place to find respite from the heat of the plains in the summer. It is only 50 kilometres from Haldwani and the last two-thirds of that section was a precipitous, steep and winding road with many hairpins leading to the mountain resort. The road was just wide enough for two vehicles, on one side was a sheer rock face and on the other a very steep drop offering no more than spaced white painted stones projecting several inches above the edge of the road surface.

Duncan was driving that dangerous road in the poor light of our lamps and, in retrospect, my comment was not confidence inspiring: 'Drive off this road and you're dead,' I said grimly but with total conviction. Duncan did not respond as he gave his entire concentration to threading his way between the white painted stones and a vast Indian truck with four lights on full beam. We had noticed already that most Indian trucks bore a huge metal quiff above their cabin and that every available surface was painted with enough psychedelic frenzy to send Picasso back to art school. They had also discovered halogen bulbs and whereas Westerners are used to dipping when they see an approaching vehicle, Indian drivers do the opposite. Their lights go on full beam with, the unmistakable message: 'Get out of my way.' Shortly afterwards we passed three vehicles, including the rally sweeper vehicle, parked precariously on the edge of the road with several people including Jingers peering ominously into the abyss. We knew that we could offer no additional help but would only add to the obstruction as we contemplated the fate of whoever had driven over the edge.

Finally, in abrupt contrast, we drove along the Mall in Nainital adjoining the peaceful lake trying to comprehend the enormity of the task of transporting a yacht to the lake in 1840. A British man requested that his yacht be taken to Nainital, despite that tough terrain having no roads, because the lake reminded him of the Lake District. We arrived one hour late, at 20.30 hours, and parked on the Flats, a level area created by an earthquake in 1880. We received a warm and enthusiastic reception from local people, augmented by a silver band, but we were anxious to check in and report Jingers' investigation at the cliff edge. The wonder of digital telephone meant that the marshals were ahead of us.

Nigel Challis, the driver of car 96, who had given us vital help with jump starts at Choksam, had found himself in a similar position to Duncan as he negotiated a tight bend on the steep road up to Nainital. He was faced by an approaching Indian truck or bus and he could not tell which as the lights, on full beam, were blinding him. He was considering how closely he dared drive his 1955 Land Rover Series 1, to the oncoming vehicle in order to avoid catching the protruding stones at the side of the road when his nearside front wheel struck one of the white painted stones and the Land Rover somersaulted over the edge. Miraculously it came to rest a mere twenty feet down on its roof in a narrow indent in the steep cliff and against a single tree. Nigel and his co-driver Anthony Jefferis, suspended upside down, had great difficult forcing open the door. When they did finally extricate themselves they could not climb the steep slope or make other competitors hear their shouts as car after car ground up the hill. Eventually they were heard and Jingers was waved down enabling him and his colleagues to rescue the two men and even winch up the Land Rover. Their survival answered their families' prayers - Anthony had only cuts and bruises whilst Nigel had a cracked vertebrae.

Chapter

10

I picked at a poor meal and stumbled into bed soon after our arrival at Nainital. We were due to check out at 8.21am on Thursday, 25th September, our twentieth day, and so I had time to find Nigel Challis before leaving. He was clearly still shaken and confirmed that his Land Rover was a write-off, remarking ruefully that the bulk of the damage occurred as it was winched out. We were allowed forty five minutes to reach our first intermediate checkpoint at Corbett Lodge and I drove purposefully down a steep hairpinned road similar to the previous evening, but in broad daylight we saw just how beautiful the scenery was. Duncan and I were both struck by a teenage Indian schoolgirl whose beauty surpassed the scenery. Roadside monkeys also distracted us and one with a very long tail shot across the road in front of us. I do not think I could have driven faster, safely and yet we still checked in sixteen minutes late at Corbett Lodge which, together with the adjoining Corbett National Park, were, in 1936, named after Jim Corbett, a British tiger hunter of some repute.

Twelve kilometres past Corbett Lodge our route book instructed us to take a tight left at a junction with a white house on the left. Everything fitted except that the house was uniformly blue and so we assumed it had been re-painted, and followed the directions. A little later we passed two filling stations on our left which were entered in the route book as being on our 'right'. We resolved not to take route book lefts and rights as gospel.

Just before we reached Kashipur, we braked to avoid a large, brown, racoon-like creature which scurried across the road in front of us. Kashipur is a considerable agricultural centre where farmers can obtain tractors and implements as well as trade their stock, but as we left the centre we started to see vehicles approaching us on our side of a dual carriageway. It was another salutary lesson in understanding the huge gap between Western and Asian standards of road discipline. Three kilometres from Moradabad two young men fought each other with furious bare fists on the roadside without a second's distraction as we swept by.

We eased on into Maradabad through a heaving mass of traffic of every description and pedestrians, and at that point we were stoned by a group of small children, but we still managed to check in on time at 12.14pm. This was the second time we had been stoned and, particularly in an open car, it produced in us the strange combination of vulnerability and aggressiveness. From this point on we were much less inclined to smile, wave and call to the crowds and much more preoccupied studying the groups of people ahead to identify the person or persons with arms raised ready to stone us. Whilst I waited for Duncan to check in the Delage I was mobbed by smiling chattering Indians. A strongly built policeman with a very confident air and a bulky swagger stick, strutted back and forth warning spectators not to crowd me too intrusively. One young man pushed in closely, smiled broadly and jabbered incomprehensibly. The smile froze and he literally leapt backwards as the policeman cracked the swagger stick across his chest.

We wove our way out of town on the last leg of the day to Delhi, for which we had an allowance of four hours twenty three minutes. We noticed the increasing number of roadside advertisements including one for 'Car loans at 10.5%'. We overtook a young man on a motor-scooter supporting seven strapped-on milk churns. We passed through Pakwada, Joya and Cayrolla and about a hundred kilometres west of Moradabad we crossed the river Ganges. Immediately on the left was a display of wickerwork for sale which stretched for several hundred metres. The number of dead dogs lying in the road had increased noticeably since arriving in India.

The traffic was not grid-locked but more swirling chaos as pedestrians and vehicles of all shapes and sizes competed energetically in all directions for every vacant inch of road. The roadside advertising was also competing but not at the same frantic level. As we neared the fifth town since crossing the Ganges, Pilkhuwa, there were extensive areas of dyed cloth drying in the fields. A large shop in the centre of the town displayed rolls of cloth of the same dyes. Shortly after the town was the proudly signed 'Jain Industrial Estate', which was followed by a chemical works as the smog reappeared on our approach to Delhi, the capital of India. In the winter, slum dwellers try to keep warm by fuelling bonfires with tyres, rags, leaves and branches, helping Delhi to retain its position as perhaps the most polluted city in the world.

Duncan suspected that we were developing a steering fault but then spotted a low, rear off-side tyre. He checked the pressure, found it was about half our normal level and decided to change to the spare wheel and have the slow puncture repaired in Delhi. He wheeled his hydraulic jack under the centre of the back axle and lifted both wheels clear of the ground in seconds. He whipped off the wheel and thrust on the spare wheel at which point the jack toppled and became wedged under the back axle. Duncan made a mental note to raise only one wheel at a time in future. It took him as long again to use a small hand jack to extract the hydraulic jack, which was damaged but still sufficiently usable to finish the job. Whilst all this industrious effort was going on I was of little help to Duncan because the heat of the northern Indian plain had suddenly got to me and I sat beneath a tree trying to recover. I sat quietly in the passenger seat continuing to recover as Duncan drove on and into the capital city of India. Delhi has fine national structures including the Rasthrapati Bhavan, the official residence of the

President of India and the famous India Gate, a forty two metre high triumphal arch and war memorial. The traffic was heavy but slightly more disciplined. There were so many pedestrians it seemed as though most of the eight hundred and fifty million population of India had turned out to welcome us. It goes some way to explain the periods of unrest in India that it has seventeen major languages in use, almost one dialect per million souls and three major religions; Hinduism encompassing Buddhism, Sikhs and Gains; Islam and Christianity. What an explosive mixture.

We checked in on time at 16.37 hours, to the luxurious Ashok Hotel. Unfortunately we were due to check out only eleven hours later on the following morning at around 3.30am on our twenty-first day. A huge elephant waited in splendid tranquillity to welcome us on the large car park in front of the hotel. We were immediately surrounded by eager journalists, photographers, television cameras and large woolly microphones. Duncan engaged in a long interview with Indian television whilst I took off the spare wheel for delivery and repair at the adjoining garage. At the end of the interview Duncan was asked, 'Do you have any message for our public?' He thought for a moment and replied: 'Yes, please ask your children not to stone us.' In spite of this blunt but perfectly understandable request, his interview was given considerable coverage on Indian television.

I normally avoid eating rice but I knew I had lost about a stone in weight and so I included rice in my dinner that evening. Even in a five star hotel I was seeking 'safe' food. From a later telephone call we learnt that there should have been roses from our wives awaiting our arrival at the Ashok Hotel, but they did not arrive in time. I went to sleep at 10pm and awoke to the alarm at 2.45am. I did not feel good - the runs had returned. We needed to travel six kilometres to India Gate to check out at 4.06am. We were in no doubt that this uncivilised start time was due to the expected Indian work to rule when we were to cross the border into Pakistan later that day. It was almost five hundred kilometres to the border and we had already been advised to try to reach it by early lunchtime. Apparently, they closed the border at 3.30pm and anyone not through by then would have to find accommodation and try again the following day. Remembering the five hours it took to get into India, it was a daunting prospect. What it meant was that we had to travel quickly even though the first three hours would be in pitch dark with little help from my headlights, which remained like flickering candles.

I always took the first stint of driving which was good because it gave me less time to think about my intestines and Duncan chance to snatch a little more sleep. I began, optimistically, thinking that we were going to drive north-west on main road No 1, a dual carriageway, and hopefully being close to Delhi, the surfaces should be better. Fortunately Duncan was asleep when I discovered the error of my thoughts. I was trying to maintain a speed of eighty kilometres but there were so many potholes I was often reduced to sixty. Worse, the Indians have the charming habit of leaving large building blocks scattered on the carriageway. Every kind of transport from bicycles through to three wheeled taxis over-loaded with up to fifteen people; slow and speedy, lit and unlit cars; lit and unlit trucks and buses; cattle being herded along the carriageway; untethered cows grazed on the narrow central reservation; and

61

pedestrians strolled across the carriageway at right angles to the traffic with as much awareness as they might muster for a country walk. There were many agricultural carts drawn by horse or oxon, with loads of crops extending well beyond the width of each cart. Scooters driven by a man often had a child on the handlebars with his wife sitting side-saddle on the pillion and holding a second child. Most vehicles poured out black diesel fumes (There are only eight traffic police officers for every 10,000 vehicles in Delhi, making exhaust-emission testing a joke!) and the huge variation in the speed of this seething mass of traffic was compounded by unceasing, clamorous noise. Unlit trucks stopped in the carriageway for drivers' tea or toilet and some were abandoned in the faster lane without warning lights. Vehicles frequently came in the opposite direction down our side of the dual carriageway and would swerve into the slow lane to avoid an abandoned truck in the fast lane. It was totally undisciplined, absolute mayhem. In the daylight it would be frightening, in the dark with poor lamps it was terrifying. On some of the other bad days I thought, 'What am I doing here, endangering myself and my only son?' Leaving Delhi in the dark was simply lethal and I believed there was little chance of all of the rally cars making it to the border without a serious incident. Duncan was still sleeping and I thought I would just have to make the best job I could of making good time in those murderous conditions.

I was alongside in the outside lane when I recognised Francesca and Jennifer's Volvo stationary on the side of the road. I felt my way over into the nearside lane and eventually stopped at the side of the road. By that time I was nearly a kilometre away from the Volvo and I decided to push on and rely on the sweep-up vehicle helping, if they were in trouble. The alternative was to join the people I had been cursing and drive the wrong way back along this side of the dual carriageway. It transpired that they had killed a dog running into the road and though they were upset and shaken they were underway again fairly quickly. I have never quite lost the feeling that I should have done more to help them.

We passed through Panipat and Pipli at reduced speeds but with no reduction in the mayhem. As the precious daylight emerged we saw a sign on the rear of a truck: 'Slow and steady wins the race,' and another on the roadside: 'Careful driving costs nothing.' Humour was seeping back to us. Another sign urged us to drive into the Kingfisher Tourist Complex just before we arrived at our first intermediate checkpoint. The Rally Association had sensibly suspended time checks for the day and were using the checkpoints as a security monitor for any missing cars. I was relieved to be on the second leg and driving in daylight. For me, the first leg from Delhi was the most dangerous drive of the rally. That nightmare journey emphasised my belief that the Peking to Paris rally was a forty three day initiative test. Nevertheless, the warmth of the Indian people was shown in their smiling welcomes as we traversed India. They sing a great deal, though their desire to sing varies inversely with their level of melodic appeal to the Western ear.

At fifty kilometres from the checkpoint we drove through Sirhind, steel city of the Punjab, and on towards Ludhiana. We saw thriving, purple-flowered, bougainvillaea in the central reservation which the French would be proud of. Ludhiana is the textile centre and very industrial but it also boasts the biggest cycle factory in the world, turning out three million cycles per annum. Phil Young thought that most of them were still on the streets of Ludhiana. We noticed that, although all Indian trucks seemed to be exotically painted to a greater or lesser degree, there seemed to be a heavy use of yellow or brownish orange colours. About fifty kilometres beyond Ludhiana we passed a small van sign written: 'Leper Society.' Another road sign in English urged, 'Slow drive, long life.' I thought it was in the wrong language. For a long time all roads seemed to be signposted to Amritsar, the last large city before the border and one with a troubled history. It was founded by the fourth Guru of the Sikhs in 1577. Its famous and beautiful Golden Temple was damaged by the Indian Army in the eighties but has now been fully restored. We arrived at the border around 2pm and again, the Indian Officials took hours to process the rally cars. The Pakistan Passport Control and Customs Officials seemed determined to show that they could be as quick as the Indians were slow and all of the rally cars passed swiftly into Pakistan, with some competitors swearing they would never set foot on Indian soil again.

We had already covered 502 kilometres on that day and we had a mere 26 kilometres to drive from the Indian border to Lahore. We arrived to find the Avari Hotel very civilised apart from having an armed guard on each landing, which we were told was for security purposes. Each competitor was handed a letter on arrival, warning against people in the street purporting to be police or government officials asking for papers. It instructed us to refer them to the hotel reception. I was again feeling overcome by the heat and it was hard to imagine the feelings of Prince Idris, driving Car 9, a 1932 Ford Model B saloon, with Richard Curtis, who, at the end of this most arduous day, found his room was double booked. It must have been the last straw but his reaction to the management ensured a speedy resolution. Robert Dean had suffered the increasing ire of Etienne Veen of car 7, over the few days prior to reaching Lahore. By discrete enquiries Robert established that Etienne was ill and suffering considerable pain. Within two days, antibiotics solved the problem for both of them.

Saturday, 27th September, the twenty-second day of the rally, was a badly needed rest day. We all felt that the Rally Association had selected rest days with care and skill. We organised the repair of another slow puncture, topped up the fuel and Duncan carried out an engine oil change. There was a good business centre on the same floor as our room and I faxed off a report to the London Evening Standard with a copy to the Derby Evening Telegraph. I had promised to relay news to the Evening Standard as a temporary reporter and in case they found it sufficiently newsworthy. Although smaller than Karachi, Lahore has been the capital of Punjab for almost 1,000 years. In the fields of art and culture it is regarded as the capital of Pakistan. The Kim's Gun of Rudyard Kipling fame is near Lahore Museum and other sights recommended were Lahore Fort, adjoining Old Lahore and the Badshahi Mosque. Minarets, or mosque towers, can give good views of the city and the Mogul Palaces are a reminder that this was once the centre of the Mogul Empire. Alas, the rest days, though well spaced, gave far too little time to view all these wonders. The Pakistan Motor Club invited all entrants to a reception and buffet supper which was appreciated even though some competitors found it rather dull. Our ladies did little to brighten the scene as they were all dressed

63

to comply with an Islamic country, including observing the Islamic hejab - the wearing of a scarf over the head - rather than to please themselves or fellow competitors. One exception was Louisa Banks who, though well covered up, at least used a light and patterned material. I was still suffering slightly from 'Delhi Belly' and so I left for an early night.

The Twenty-third day of the rally, Sunday, 28th September, gave us a more comfortable start time of 9.20am. My stomach was worse and I was feeling very fatigued, probably due to loss of minerals. I took Enterosan and Dioralyte to try to counteract the problems. It was a shaky start but we only had a day of 343 kilometres to reach Multan. It was an area where grinding poverty prevailed and we observed far less audience reaction. Life expectancy in Pakistan is only about 58 years and there was little sign of joie de vivre amongst those plodding through their life span. Almost half of the Pakistan roads are unpaved but, as we crossed the lower Punjab, for most of the time we simply needed to avoid potholes. Half way between Manga and Pattoki we saw a man dressed in green, including his turban, and waving a green flag. The colour green is a traditional symbol of Islam. An unconnected variant of green was an extensive garden centre just west of Pattoki. We made the first intermediate time check on time and Duncan ate a light lunch but I could only face a Coke.

At about 150 kilometres from Lahore we saw a fertiliser warehouse and a Massey Ferguson dumper in use. The most easterly Massey Ferguson? Soon after, in Sahiwal a camel pulling a cart reminded us that the surface of dumper selling was only scratched. The camel was being beaten by a man wielding a stick but to little effect. We reached our second time check on time and set out on the final leg of 63 kilometres, passing Pakarab Fertilisers en-route and again arriving on time at 16.13 hours at the Holiday Inn in Multan. I missed dinner as well as lunch and had my one and only consultation with the Rally doctor, Greg Williams. He was convinced that my second bout of illness was due to a virus and that it would keep recurring unless I took antibiotics. A course of four tablets per day of Ciproxin was necessary for three days but he only had four tablets left. He gave me those and suggested I ask around my fellow competitors to see if they had any from their own supply, which they could spare for me. 'You were all told it was essential to have them with you,' he admonished. I asked a selection of competitors but no-one had them, or had heard of Ciproxin or the direction to include them in their medical kit.

Chapter

11

I awoke with the alarm at 5.00am on 29th September feeling a little better but part of the doctor's advice was not to eat till that evening - even though I had missed meals on 28th. I knew it was going to be a tough day because we had to cover almost twice the distance of the previous day - 624 kilometres - with three intermediate stops. It was rumoured that the Rally Association wanted to organise a day which would 'sort the wheat from the chaff.' It was also the only day when we would travel for almost 200 kilometres without a map. The Rally Association has specified eighteen maps which were needed for the rally, but on that day we needed a nineteenth map because there was a large loop of road which simply went off the map. We hoped that the route book for this section in particular would not include printed directions which were opposite to the ones intended by the organisers. To add to our concern the loop was almost certain to be driven in the dark. We were warned also that the Multan to Quetta road near the Afghanistan border was one of the most dangerous roads in the world, teeming with armed bandits, previously trained to counter the snipers of Afghanistan.

It was going to be a hot day but through varied and interesting country. At the beginning of our first leg we again passed through an area of great deprivation and glancing at the wretched hovels we were passing in this arid country, I remarked to Duncan: 'Isn't it a lucky accident of birth to be born in a beautiful, prosperous and free country like England?' His response was vehemently positive with underlying gratitude, not to me but for his sheer good fortune. There is nothing each of us can do to influence our place of birth; for each of us it is an accidental happening. To be born in a deprived, British inner city may not be fortunate but the new arrival must have a hugely greater chance of breaking out of deprivation than a new-born arriving in a remote, arid and desolate part of Asia.

I went on musing about the other lucky accidents of birth - to be born with average or better intelligence; to be born to comfortable or even wealthy parents; to be born with robust good health; and to be born with a comfortable balance of hormones. A fortunate minority enjoy all these lucky accidents of birth, but how many consider their counterparts born into miserable poverty in remote and backward countries or born in the right place, but with low intelligence or feeble health? These differences are as lucky or unlucky as a throw of the dice. That is why the less fortunate deserve the help and consideration of the more fortunate. In our crossing of Asia we had yet to see a deformed or disabled person, yet in our cities they would be visible on a daily basis. How do they achieve it? Is it their diet? Do they hide them? Do they kill them?

It is hard to reconcile whole Asian families housed in one room with the current climate of opinion about housing in Britain. It is said that the number of new houses 'required' in Britain involves the equivalent of building ten new cities the size of Bristol. Can you imagine how that would decimate the beauty and relative peace of the British Isles? So why do we need ten, new, large cities? Is it because of growth of population? No, our population is close to static, it is because a much larger proportion of people wish to be alone in the occupation of a house. We have to think again, our government must think again. Leaving aside the moral and social correctitude of one person, one house, the price of ruining our beautiful homeland is too great. So more power to our Prime Minister in his personal opposition to attacks on the Green Belt.

My musing had taken us to 50 kilometres and we were moving into semi-desert. The Ghazigat Bridge, built in 1984, took us over the Indus River and eventually to our first time check at Sakh Sarwar - a mere two minutes late. A row of wooden beds were under a low roof and I lay next to Jan Dunkley taking a short break. My health was at a low point and I felt wretched. The second section to Fort Munro was only 45 kilometres but we were only allowed forty six minutes. Most of it was an uphill mountain route and, where long sections of new road were being constructed, we were taken completely off road and often along bumpy river beds. Much of the surface was sand or gravel and, once again, I believed that I would have taken longer than forty six minutes to negotiate it in my new Range Rover. On the way we lost a blow-up cushion which the navigator used regularly to snatch sleep as the other drove and eventually we checked in at 11.22am - an hour and a quarter late. We were then told by the marshal that for some unexplained reason another forty five minutes had been added to the time allowed and so we were only half an hour late. A further discrepancy caused the marshals to insist that we could not start the third leg for another hour, even though we still had 450 kilometres of driving to Quetta.

It was clear that the drivers of some of the younger, classic cars, were making a considerable effort to meet the tight schedule. Cars careered into the forecourt of Fort Munro and I was just thinking 'This is an accident waiting to happen,' when Josef Feit in car 72, a 1967 Volkswagen Cabriolet, almost collided with our stationary Delage. His son, René Feit, who had celebrated his eighteenth birthday the day before, leapt out of the car, checked in and climbed back in as the Volkswagen took off on the third leg.

We had been warned about the heat and advised to take four litres of water per person for each day. I was still starving myself, I had no appetite but I was drinking lots of water. Geoffrey Dorey, driving car 45, a 1960 Morris Minor, with his wife, Jennie, was feeling extremely hot. To relieve his discomfort Jennie placed a wet towel over Geoffrey's head. Unfortunately the towel slipped over his eyes and the Morris weaved off the road into the desert and back again before Geoffrey could remove it. Fortunately, there was no damage and, though there is no doubt that wet towels help in excessively hot weather, the application is important! When we were about 20 kilometres into the third leg a man at the roadside stood placidly with a hawk on his wrist and soon afterwards an eighteen inch reptile scurried across in front of the Delage. Then my soap bag which I had forgotten to re-stow fell out of the car but I heard it fall and we were able to recover it. A sand and gravel extraction plant was operating and I wondered how they chose where to begin as sand and gravel seemed to be everywhere. Duncan said that he understood that .03% of the world's surface was covered in tarmac but it seemed that Pakistan did not have its share.

We reached Loralai, our third time check, at 16.59 hours, an hour and thirty nine minutes late. The police had re-diverted the rally around Loralai where we had intended to refuel and so at the beginning of the last leg we made for a filling station about seven kilometres out. We were dismayed to find that it had run out of fuel. Although it was becoming dusk and we still had 260 kilometres to go, we had no choice but to retrace the road to Loralai. The policeman re-directing the rally traffic was also coping with milling crowds of spectators. By sign language we showed that fuel was low and he directed us vaguely into the centre. I persuaded a spectator to ride on our running board and direct us and I think it unlikely we would have found it without him. All the way there and back he was calling and waving proudly to friends.

To add to our mounting unease we were stoned again as we left Loralai and as we drove out, our side lights fused. We later heard that some competitors had given up for the day and found overnight accommodation in Loralai. Driving into the darkness our only guidance was the route book, which I became increasingly convinced was inaccurate and too sparse. In one case there was a 63 kilometres gap between directions. We had also been warned to beware of sandstorms, but mercifully we did not suffer those as well. Driving on a long but narrow, straight stretch of road I saw the single headlight of what I assumed was a motorcycle approaching from some distance. We were about thirty feet apart and closing at a speed of at least 100 kilometres when I realised that the single headlight was a car's nearside lamp and I saw the unlit offside lamp centred on my radiator. We both swerved violently and passed within an inch of each other. Another unquantifiable shortening of my life span.

We came to a fork in the road with no signpost or direction and with no reference to it in the route book. We had not seen another rally car for hours but I felt we had to consider which way to go rather than taking a fifty : fifty chance. It was scary. At that point Prince Idris in car 9 drew alongside and I was mightily relieved that we could share the decision with Idris and his co-driver, Richard Curtis. We quickly decided to fork right and to stick with each other until we were either back in an area where we had a map or at least the route book related to the road we travelled. It was certainly valuable for cars 9 and 10 to drive as a team whilst we were in mapless, directionless, territory.

I asked Idris to take the lead as his headlamps were much better than mine and I drove about fifty yards behind him. After about an hour we were driving along an appalling gravel road of no more than four metres in width through black wilderness. Duncan was sleeping and we had not seen another vehicle, other than car 9, since our meeting at the fork in the road. I was immediately aware when another set of headlights appeared behind me. The car behind began the usual hooting urging me to pull over and let him pass. I edged a little closer to car 9 and moved over as close as I dared to the unmarked edge of that narrow road. The overtaking car was a small pick-up truck and the occupants of its two seats peered across at me as it hovered alongside the Delage. I could not understand his delay in sweeping past me and then Car 9, as Idris's headlamps revealed a straight road ahead and then suddenly the pick-up pulled sharply and diagonally in front of me and the driver stood on his brakes.

In the split second of my emergency braking and swerving to avoid him I was in no doubt that this was an attempt to hi-jack the Delage by splitting it from its coupling with Car 9, which could be hundreds of metres away before Idris realised we were no longer following. I immediately accelerated and slipped into the narrow gap between the pick-up's bonnet and the nearside of the road. Duncan awoke with a start as the Delage brakes locked on and looked to his left in horror as I accelerated with my near-side wheels on the road edge. His shout was almost a scream: 'What the hell are you doing? You're going to break an axle.' My wordless response was to swing back into the centre of the road and close up on Car 9. The pick-up driver was not pleased, either because his first attempt at hi-jacking had failed or because he was astounded that a Western driver should re-overtake on the inside.

He positioned the pick-up right on my tail and hooted incessantly whilst I baulked him by hugging the middle of the road, to Duncan's increasing bewilderment and irritation. The spectacle of his father's seemingly irrational behaviour convinced him that his dad's imagination had taken over and he had lost his senses. Whilst holding off the pick-up I said tensely: 'I think he is trying to hi-jack us and he may have a gun.' Duncan looked at me incredulously.

'Rubbish, he's just an ordinary Pakistani trying to overtake and if he has a gun the way you're baulking him could encourage him to use it.' I did not reply as I focused on the straight road ahead of Car 9 and reduced my distance behind Idris to two metres before easing over to allow the pick-up to overtake. It seemed to have assumed a menacing personality of its own as it pulled alongside and again hovered, but the driver saw the two metre gap I was still maintaining and swept on past Car 9, never to be seen again by either of us. I then responded tersely to Duncan:

'That could mean that he was just an innocent local driver but we shall never know. He could have been a thwarted hi-jacker. He made the classic move to forcibly separate two cars and in that split second I believed it was a hi-jack attempt. I was driving and it was my decision - you were asleep anyway. When you're driving it's your decision.' Duncan grudgingly admitted that the passenger did seem to be holding a rifle and we relapsed into seething silence. Shortly afterwards my beloved hat blew off and I opted to abandon it. When we were back on the map and fast approaching Quetta, I left Idris re-fuelling in a Shell station - by agreement and with a fond farewell.

After seventeen hours of travelling at just after midnight, we pulled into the car park of the Hotel Quetta Serena. Werner was waiting anxiously and greeted us with relief but also with tragic news. Josef and René Feit's Volkswagen had collided with a stationary bus in Quetta just a kilometre short of reaching our hotel. René was killed outright and Josef died in hospital soon after. It was an appalling end to a day which had severely tested all the participants, but at least the others had survived. We parked the car and wearily extracted the essentials for an overnight stay and made secure the rest. As we were doing this we were jostled by journalists and locals wanting photographs. I responded testily to questions and was jolted by one question from a Pakistani: 'Are you pissed off?'

'What do you mean?', was my startled reply.

'Are you pissed off because your friends have been killed?'

'Of course I'm pissed off, who wouldn't be?' 'Pissed off' was not a phrase I would have chosen to relate to the deaths, but it was more a reaction to his question.

'Do you blame us?', he persisted.

'No of course not,' I replied in astonishment, 'this is a rally and it can be dangerous. No-one is to blame.' He seemed mollified but still persisted:

'Are you English?'

'Yes.'

'What is your name?'

'I think you have asked me enough questions, were you trying to trap me into some kind of admission? Go and ask the Rally Association.'

'I was just trying to help you.'

'It's very kind of you and that I do appreciate,' I replied in warmer tones, but terminating the conversation.

The tragedy cast a pall over the rally and although Phil Young offered all competitors the opportunity to take a rest day in Quetta instead of Zahedan, all but a few soldiered on the following morning. It was 12.14am when we checked into the Hotel Quetta Serena, almost two hours late on the last leg of the day. Duncan declined to eat and went straight to bed in order to squeeze in four hours sleep - we were due to start at 6.19am. I had eaten nothing for forty eight hours and for the first time in that miserable period, I felt slightly hungry. I persuaded the chef to organise Chicken Maryland for me and gave up an hour of precious sleep to eat it. The rally doctor was sitting at an adjoining table and I told him that no competitors had any of the appropriate antibiotics, never mind spare ones. He said he would look into it the following morning but I never heard from him again. Fortunately, I rose at four o'clock feeling much better and had no further re-occurrence of the dreaded Delhi-Belly. After that seventeen hour drive and the awful news on arrival we added a new expletive to our vocabulary 'Quetta!'

Chapter

12

We puzzled over a small oil leak after breakfast but Werner was in like a flash to tighten the offending bolt so that we were only a little late leaving at 6.45am. The police redirected the rally out of town, missing the filling stations - one of which we had planned to use for a complete refill of the tank before setting off through Pakistani desert. One filling station remained on our route at about 30 kilometres from Quetta and we were confident we still had enough fuel to make it. We did, but to our dismay it was again the petrol equivalent of the pub with no beer. We had a serious problem. The last thing we wanted to do was to retrace our route to Quetta when we had 724 kilometres to reach Zahedan following the route of Marco Polo through serious desert and in very hot weather. Yet we had only two jerry cans of petrol which would cover a maximum of 160 kilometres unless we could find unofficial sources of petrol with all its possibilities of being stored in dirty cans, watered down, stolen or over-priced.

We decided to take a big risk, push on westwards and hope to find unofficial sources of petrol frequently enough. We tipped in the two jerry cans and set off. I had plenty of thoughts to take my mind off running out of fuel in the middle of the desert. What a waste to have passed through Quetta with little observation. It was largely rebuilt in 1935 after an earthquake which killed 20,000 people. It is a fertile oasis in an arid mountainous area, yet it is a frontier fortress town being the hub of roads to Afghanistan, India and Persia. The road surface was better and I was able to look around more. I saw a camel with front legs tied together and another camel appearing to herd goats in the manner of a dog. We passed the occasional ancient fort and the odd military pill box. There were regular points for collecting Chagia levies but we were never asked to pay. A railway closely followed the road through inhospitable country and the road frequently crossed the railway.

We recognised the unofficial fuel stations in the small, one street, desert villages by looking for jerry cans under a lean-to roof or by asking a local person to point it out. We made several stops at these dubious but vital 'filling stations'. Each stop caused great excitement locally and the petrol was poured through our filtered funnel from battered jerry cans by ragged young boys. The amount of fuel we purchased was usually governed by their supply rather than our capacity. At one stop under a cloudless blue sky, the ambient temperature was 105° Fahrenheit.

We were about to top up our behind-the-seat water supply from the secure compartment when we discovered that the thinner polythene bottles, with which we had recently re-stocked, had all burst under the weight of packing. We were down to a half litre bottle of water between us and in the desert heat we were forced to buy six bottles of Coke at a time. We had our time card stamped at the first checkpoint, Desert Road, even though after yesterday's disaster the Rally Association had dropped the time checks for the day. Just before Desert Road the film crew were travelling directly behind us with the camera trained on the back of the Delage. The cameraman remarked to his colleague that our off-side rear tyre looked a bit low, whereupon we had a dramatic blow-out. They were able to take some real action footage as it looked as though we were losing a wheel. We quickly swapped the damaged tyre for the spare, after we had declined the film crew's offer of help and they raced off in search of more action. The café at Desert Road had a pick-up truck with a machine gun mounted on the back standing in its car park. Several competitors, including Duncan and Adam Hartley, climbed onto the back to be photographed with the gun. I spoke to the man who had invited them up and found that he and his colleagues were a special plain-clothed police group operating as a mobile anti-drug unit intercepting drugs from Afghanistan and Pakistan to Turkey.

Another 120 kilometres took us through real desert to the second checkpoint at Dalbandin. On the way we had long spells of travelling with no other vehicles in view and with the golden sand blowing and partly obscuring the road. Not the place to break down. After Dalbandin we had almost 300 kilometres to reach the border between Pakistan and Iran but fortunately the Government were building a long straight dual carriageway to connect with the border. Many sections were unusable or even required an off-road diversion but whenever possible the rally cars were directed onto the unopened road to use long stretches. It was new tarmacadam and we could cruise at 80-90 kilometres. Surrounding the new road was arid 'gravel car parks' as far as the eye could see. A number of cars had disappeared into back street garages for repairs to their suspension but Gerry Acher driving car 4, a 1932 Aston Martin, was more fortunate when he was delayed. He was served tea and biscuits and later dinner with the District Commissioner in his oasis garden in the middle of the desert.

We were thirsty all of the time and passing through salt flats did not help us to think of things other than thirst. We were driving through a desolate landscape but with distant mountains framing a beautiful sunset when our rear mudguard stay fell off in two parts. Duncan backed up and collected them. We reached the border at about five thirty pm and found that, as usual in Asia, no-one other than villainous looking money touts, wanted to know about changing notes from the country one was leaving. We built up a growing stock of Asian currencies which were unchangeable and only usable in the country of the currency. We were also warned that there was a real danger of being mugged in the no-man's land between the Pakistan and Iran borders. We left the

71

Pakistan frontier driving behind Howard Bellm and Christopher Taylor who drove their 1968 Chevrolet Camaro with surging panache through no-man's land, even though their circuitous route convinced us they had not taken in the directions which were as vague as the route itself.

Our welcome at the Iranian border was excellent. We were given flowers and presents, led through passport and customs speedily and directed to a nearby filling station for free petrol. The free petrol was available throughout Iran, courtesy of the Car Club of Iran. Don Jones had his passport and carnet stolen in Tibet but managed to smile and laugh his way through the borders up to Iran. A very serious Iranian official was contemplating the gravity of the missing documents when Don burst into his rendition of, 'I Left My Heart in San Francisco'. The startled official smiled and waved Don through. Duncan was taking a fast ride on Western-type roads which even had cats-eyes and white lines, when we were startled to be insistently waved by the police into their checkpoint. Their only purpose was to give us free bottles of water, fruit juice and more flowers. It was ironic that having spent a mere few hours at the excellent Hotel Quetta Serena we were to spend thirty-six hours, including a rest day, in the Zahedan Tourist Hotel. After the warm welcome at the border and from the austerely dressed ladies on arrival, the hotel was very disappointing. The bathrooms were very poor with stand up toilets. Dinner was unappetising and the staff's refusal of our jocular requests for alcohol was rather zealous but no objection was raised when I smoked my cigar.

We heard that the rally leader had changed that day, for the first time since leaving Beijing. John and Simon Catt in car 50, a 1965 Ford Cortina Mark 1, fell back from first to third place and car 97, a 1942 Ford Willys Jeep MB, driven by John Bayliss with Phil Surtees, had taken the lead. John Van der Laan and Willem Graal driving car 43, a 1958 Citroën 2CV, were less fortunate. They drove off the road damaging their front suspension and dropped back to twenty sixth place.

The Rally Association described Zahedan as a small, dusty town and I think it was vastly accurate. There was no pool at the hotel and neither its daytime or evening atmosphere gave much hope of a party. It was, therefore, less of a hardship to be engaged for most of the day repairing the broken bits on the Delage. Dinner that evening was another turgid affair, with indifferent food and our ladies smarting under the tyrannical eye of the female overseer, whose role seemed to be to protect the people of the Islamic Republic of Iran from the indiscretions of Western visitors. Carolyn Ward, driving a 1961 Land Rover Series 11A with David Tremain, later told us an amusing story about the Iranian attitude to ladies. Carolyn found they would not accept a woman's authority for even minor things - they insisted that her husband must approve them. She overcame this by asking the amicable Howard Bellm to pose as her assumed husband and 'approve' an order for an oil change and payment of a laundry bill. After dinner I asked the waiter if I could have coffee but he said it was too late. When I asked for hot water to add to my own Nescafé he referred me to the female overseer in a nearby office. My curiosity made me pursue this charade. She took me to the surly head waiter who produced some cold water. I asked again for hot water but he said: 'No. Too late.'

Without coffee but with my cigar I was joined in the sparsely furnished foyer by a local who introduced himself as a sports coach at the local college. His speciality was martial arts and he disclosed casually that he held seventeen black belts. He seemed a charming man but I avoided controversial subjects and slipped off to bed at 10.30pm. I slept soundly, awoke to the alarm at 5.00am and left promptly at 7.17am for the first leg of a 558 kilometres drive to Kerman. The road was fast and we reminded ourselves to drive on the right again, at times cruising near our maximum speed of 100 kilometres. On both sides of the road the desert was so desolate that we covered 122 kilometres before we saw the first flock of sheep. The vegetation was so sparse and spaced that one could believe that 100 acres might be needed to sustain one sheep. At 140 kilometres from Zahedan the scenery changed to beautiful mountainous terrain before crossing the Dasht e Lut, a hot, remote and bleak, area.

We reached the first checkpoint early at 9.48am, Desert Café, but that time we were allowed to leave early without penalty. Soon we were watching a lone camel crossing a 'gravel car park' and on the left we passed a three hundred year old tower built to help travellers find their way. The desert became interspersed with rocks and small copses. Then came a further improvement in soil fertility as we saw a number of fruit farms but 20 kilometres further on we were back to the 'gravel car park'. We passed a railway under construction at 310 kilometres, Bam Airport at 340 kilometres and a power station at 345 kilometres. The new railway is to join Zahedan to Kerman - the only missing link in a continuous railway between Europe and China.

We arrived at the Arg E Bam checkpoint early and took a break to look at the old walled city of Arg E Bam. Much of it dates back to the twelfth century and it is said that an early conqueror occupied the city and put out the eyes of all its 20,000 inhabitants. Presumably he committed this hideous assault to gain power over the newly enslaved people but, apart from his wickedness, I think his judgement was questionable too as blinded people would be of limited service. We climbed to the top of the city wall over the only entrance and surveyed the myriad ruined mud-brick houses divided by narrow streets. Some restoration work was being done but it still resembled Pompeii without the solidified larva. Duncan and I were discussing and trying to imagine 20,000 people thronging the city in its prime when another competitor hailed us, glanced at the litre bottle of water I was carrying, thrust out his hand, grasped the bottle, unscrewed the top and took a long drink only just preceded by: 'May I take a drink from your bottle'. I would have thought twice about such behaviour even if I were gasping in the middle of a desert rather than in a desert town.

We made good time in the afternoon and the temperature cooled as we climbed to reach Kerman at an altitude of about 6,000 feet by about 4pm. It was early enough for a welcome swim but the pool looked uninvitingly green. However, the bathrooms were a great improvement on the previous evening. Before dinner we catalogued our current list of repairs required. We had broken brackets to be welded for the offside petrol tank stay and the near-side running board and wing stay. The petrol tank stay was made slightly less serious because it was resting on a strong protective tray to avoid the tank being pierced by a rock. In addition, the engine was missing in the mid-range of revs;

nevertheless we decided not to try and cram the repairs in that evening but to limp through the next day to Esfahan and once again, use our 'rest day' on repairs.

We left Kerman at 7.18am on our twenty-eighth day with 675 kilometres to drive and we were soon back in the desert, relieved only by the occasional oasis or village. At 100 kilometres we passed through Rafsangan, named after their famous resident, President Rafsangan and shortly afterwards we drove around a dead mule in the road - the first we saw killed on the whole trip. Then another first, a lone, cycling, bearded Westerner, pedalling steadily eastwards. He was either a very brave man or psychologically beyond reality (nuts). We continued driving into so much haze it was almost fog and glancing around at the monotonous desert I remarked that it would need a soil analyst to discern any variation in the landscape rolling by. Duncan nodded but made no attempt to expand on the thought. For a high proportion of the time we were comfortable in each others company, sometimes conversing energetically and sometimes deep in our own thoughts not needing to break the silence or feeling uncomfortable with it.

We checked in on time at 13.07 hours in Mehriz and then on the second leg the road ran between the Dasht e Lut sand desert on the left and the Dasht e Kavir salt desert on the right (north). We passed the Zoroastrian Towers of Silence on our right - relic of an old religious custom where the dead were left on a hill to be picked clean by the vultures whilst their relatives stayed respectfully for several days. After passing through Nain with its carpet-making and its mosque originating in the tenth century, we rose steadily into the mountains seeing three mixed flocks of sheep and goats and a fruit farm, completely enclosed by a protective wall illustrating once again the Asian technique of building a large rectangular compound with a high security wall and a single entrance - in effect a private fort or commune area. How the contents of the compound were made up almost seemed to be an afterthought, ie. whether they would house buildings, crops, or simply be safe housing for beasts or implements.

Driving a straight road through this dry arid country, it is surprising to contemplate that even as much as seven or eight percent of it is covered by trees and that thirty percent of its boundaries are seacoast. To the north the Caspian Sea, the world's largest inland water basin and source of the famous Persian caviar, is linked to the Black Sea via The Volga-Don Canal. To the south, the Persian Gulf and Oman Sea give strategic importance to Iran, as the bulk of the world's crude oil production is exported through the Strait of Hormoz. Although individually, the people are generous and hospitable, the Government is religionary and repressive and it is surprising that such bigoted control can be maintained over a people with such diverse languages and culture. Less than half of the population speak the official language, Farsi (Persian), and how can the Government draw into the main stream of national life such minority groups as, for example, the semi-nomadic tribes inhabiting the western mountains?

We were stoned again before dropping back down to the 'gravel car park' type of desert but with some scattered industrial plants including a pipe works with a railway siding. About 25 kilometres short of Esfahan we called at a filling station to fill our tank. It was not one of the stations organised by the Iran Auto Club and so we had to pay in cash, but we were surprised that the cost equated to 20p per gallon - cheaper than a can of Coke! Cultivated fields appeared increasingly and finally, we reached our overnight resting point, the Abbasi Hotel in Esfahan on time at 1935 hours.

Esfahan is in the most populated area of Iran, but was as close as we were allowed to pass immediately south of Teheran, the capital city with its population of ten million. Esfahan is an interesting city with a river not unlike the Avon winding through Stratford with its tree-lined, low, grassy, flat banks and an impressive five hundred year old bridge. The Abbasi Hotel was converted from a traditional caravanserai and built around a huge courtyard with a fine chaykhune (tea garden), built in the form of a recess from the courtyard and having a high domed ceiling. Tea could be taken whilst lounging on a chaise-long and puffing at a water pipe, all prepared by a courteous attendant. For me it was unrivalled as the most peaceful place in Iran.

As soon as we had dropped our baggage in our room we went to meet with members of the Iran Auto Club to discuss arrangements for the following (rest) day and, specifically, where to go to have a new support bracket made for our fuel tank. We intended to fix a time to meet and then go straight in for dinner but they persuaded us to go with them immediately to a workshop about fifteen minutes drive away. Whilst the mechanics were making a new bracket, Preacher, a friendly member of the Auto Club who had accompanied us, expressed his concern about the whittled plugs which Duncan had used to plug the leaks on both sides of the fuel tank. He thought the drips were too frequent and that he could mix up a recipe to seal them from dates and other Iranian ingredients. When he had finished making his potion he picked up a hammer and gave each plug several hard thumps to knock them flush with the ends of the supporting pipes, before applying the sticky potion all around the ends. We fitted on the newly fashioned bracket, hoisted the fuel tank back into its correct position and drove back to the secure car park close to the Abbasi Hotel.

Duncan did his habitual check for leaking petrol before leaving the car. A large pool of petrol was expanding rapidly under the rear of the car. We were dismayed and frustrated by yet another episode in the petrol leak saga. Preacher, a tall, handsome and normally cheerful man, was also dismayed. It was almost midnight and too late for any further work and he suggested dejectedly that we parked the Delage in the remotest part of the car park to quarantine it from healthy cars and then dismantle and take the petrol tank away from the car the following morning, fill it with water and try to weld the leaks. We trudged back to the Abbasi having missed dinner completely and taken our car decidedly backwards in terms of road-worthiness. I cursed my stupidity for standing by and watching Preacher belting away at the wooden plugs with his hammer. There was no doubt in my mind that the hammering had opened up the split in the supporting tube still more and that no amount of plugs or potion would stop the flow.

We breakfasted early on Saturday, 4th October, then spent from 9.00am until 8pm of our fatuously entitled 'rest day' in the same workshop as the previous evening. Whilst the tank was being disconnected and removed to the welding shop we managed to repair the headlamp and running board bracket. The gaping hole where the fuel tank used to be revealed that the rear, off-side auxiliary spring was misplaced at its base and so we were able to reinstate it. It was a bonus to have spotted it because it would soon have distorted and broken and we had no spare.

Preacher and his fellow club members drove us back to the Abbasi and organised an excellent relaxed lunch. I wanted to be their host as some small recognition of their kindness and persistence but they would not hear of it. Before returning to the dreaded workshop, they took us to the Chaykhume overlooking the hotel courtyard. For a blissful half hour we drank tea and smoked the water pipes. The newly welded tank was reassembled and re-fitted but when we parked in the secure car park that evening, disappointingly, it was still dripping once every five seconds. We turned our backs on the Delage, ate a modest dinner al fresco in the courtyard with a smiling, welcoming Sylvia Esch, and then took her to share our second tranquil visit to the Chaykhume.

Nepalese labourer   *Life alongside the Ganges*

Psychedelic Indian truck

8 rivers down, 5 to go in Nepal

Amphibious car 77

Story time

Converging spectators

Indian family on scooter

300 year old watching tower in the desert

Over-burdened camel

Pakistani desert

Clearing desert sand from Pakistani road

Walled city of Arg E Bam

Delage petrol tank removed for welding in Esfahan

The Chaykhume at the Abbasi Hotel in Esfahan

Mount Ararat where Noah's Ark was stranded !

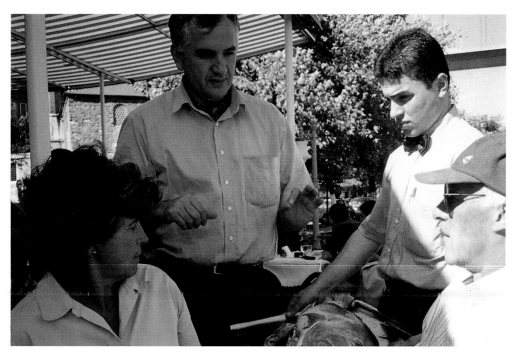

Celebration lunch at the Iskele Restaurant, Istanbul

Flying monasteries of Metéora, Greece

Repairing broken spring leaf outside Greek McDonald's

Fog in the Austrian Alps

Repairing broken spring leaf, for second time, in Reims

Joy and relief at the Paris Finish

My boys are back !

Chapter

13

Once again our desire to experience the atmosphere and see the buildings which make up this historical city was subordinated by the need to maintain the Delage as an active participant in the rally. In 1612 the Meidun e Emain, one of the largest squares in the world, was built in Esfahan. Polo used to be played in the square and the goals are still in place. The sumptuous mosque with its intricate tilework was built at an angle to the square so that it faced Mecca. A huge bazaar also fronts the square, which we approached in heavy traffic, diverse and undisciplined by Western standards. In extreme contrast, the Sunday Times of 18th January, 1998, reported that, not far north of Esfahan, the Iranians were within the turn of a screwdriver of completing an atomic bomb.

We rose at 5am on our thirtieth day for a 7.16am start and were soon climbing through an arid plain but with green mountains forming the horizon on both sides of the road. Small isolated copses began to appear and I did not expect to see magpies or evidence of pigeon fanciers - a pigeon loft - in Iran, but they were there. At around 70 kilometres we saw the symbol of the Islamic Republic emphatically marked on the hillside. The soil was still arid and I wondered how many millions of acres would be needed there to equal the production of one thousand acres of arable land in Lincolnshire, but the number of trees and small copses was increasing. Twenty kilometres on was a power station and a further twenty kilometres took us, on time, to the first time check of the day, Gholpayagen.

At around 200 kilometres a hawk performed its isolated, ruthless reconnoitre. At 230 kilometres we entered Khomein. There was a little confusion because the map still showed it as Homein but clearly it was re-named in tribute to it being the birthplace of the late, Islamic fundamentalist leader, Ayatollah Khomeini, founder of the Islamic Republic of Iran in 1979. Khomein was the only town in Iran where we received an aggressive reception from the crowd. Presumably it is the epicentre of Islamic fever and anti-Western feeling, being the seed of the Republic. The aggression was anticipated by the Iran Auto Club members, who stood at strategic points on our route through the town, urging us to keep moving as swiftly as was possible with safety. As if to emphasis their concern I saw a young man in the throng tear out flowers from a bed in the central reservation and then hurl it into my face. I was too slow to avoid the impact and along with the flowers, I received the roots and a good deal of the soil. I had soil in both eyes and it was also scattered around the inside of the car. I did not see much of the remainder of Khomein as I washed out my eyes with eye drops but we were relieved to see it receding in our side mirrors.

At 235 kilometres we passed another power station and saw an increasing number of industrial plants. We followed the ring road around the large commercial centre of Arak and from then on it became busier with more frequent towns and villages. Around 300 kilometres we were surprised to see six storey apartments and a new residential estate - more Western-like than anything we had passed further east. This was followed by fairly new one, two and three storey housing built in what looked like common bricks. They were inexpressibly ugly and it was sad to see a human contribution so devoid of aesthetics, especially placed in a rugged mountain setting. Even in that more urban setting it was clear that the occupiers still called for layouts which recognised their high awareness of security needs. Twenty kilometres further on a large refinery on our left had been a major and conspicuous target for Iraq in their recent war with Iran. Our second time check of the day was reached on time. We refilled the tank and were beginning to pass ploughed fields when a truck trundled by carrying a desert tank. Our kilometer recorded the ten thousandth kilometre of the rally and soon after a day's total of 500 kilometres we reached Hamadan. At 1,750 metres above sea level, Hamadan attracts Iranians escaping from summer heat. It is reputed to be one of the oldest continuously inhabited towns in the world. It was a resting place on the route to Baghdad and some of its tombs date back to the fifth century A.D.

We drove into Hamadan along a dual carriageway and into a blinding sunset. Frequently 'black shrouded, suicide maidens', as Duncan termed them, strolled across the carriageway, seemingly indifferent to the fast moving traffic, which approached with seriously impeded vision. We parked near to the headquarters hotel, although for once we were not booked in there but were bussed to a nearby and better hotel. Before leaving the car we had recorded that the dripping petrol had increased to one per second. Supper, cigar and bed by 9pm, were in short order as we needed our alarm call at 4.0am. We then had to leave on a 5.30am bus for a 6.26am start. We drove along good, though winding roads and after about 130 kilometres, through beautiful rolling countryside at a height of 5,000 feet or more. It was much like Salisbury Plain on a fine but hazy day with a much cooler temperature and we increasingly passed cultivated land. We reached Sarifabad time check on time, admired its fine old bridge and continued through the Salisbury-like plain, now fringed by mountains. Soon after leaving Sarifabad we motored continuously through a short dust storm in a funnelled valley.

We reached the second time check of the day on time, Maiinbolagh, which at 2,300 metres was the highest point of our route through Iran. We were stoned again but thwarted other attempts by identifying potential assailants and gesturing aggressively with an accusing finger and shouting 'No.' Sad, but better than a cut head, broken windscreen or headlamps. We then began to descend for a while on a more twisty road. Later we saw a mule-drawn covered wagon which seemed to be directly from the Wild West. At 470 kilometres we had a fine view of a lake but after 500 kilometres it became more industrial with sightings of pipeworks, a power station, an oil refinery and a business park. It was industrial strip development. Near the end of our 565 kilometres day, as often happened, I became effectively saddle-sore. Even with the camping blow-up pillows it was difficult to get comfortable. We arrived on time at the International Hotel in Tabriz, which is an industrial and commercial city renowned for carpet-making, silverware, jewellery and spices. Although Tabriz was the Persian capital for a while, its buildings have a more Russian than Asian appearance.

Our petrol leak had now again increased its pace to such an extent that we had to delay refuelling till just before our start at 5.42am the following morning. One of the half dozen rumours about the nearby garage was that it was open all night - we hoped that one was correct. Duncan attached plastic metal to various places on the tank and support to try to curb the drips. We went to bed at 10pm in anticipation of an alarm call five and a half hours later. After breakfast, I filled up with fuel and Duncan checked out and joined me at the nearby filling station for our thirty-second start, on Tuesday, 7th October. We inspected Duncan's plastic metal and found it was still soft. We set out to find our way out of the city in pitch dark and in the first rain storm on our rally for some time. I recalled that on guard duty during my National Service, I had vowed to myself that after returning to civilian life, I would never subject myself to anything more active than sleep during the early hours of the morning. We drove past a large truck terminal in the industrial outskirts of what was undoubtedly a strategic city with its proximity to Iraq, Turkey and the former USSR. Soon we were crossing a large arid plain, though with some areas of cultivation and encircled by mountains. After about 100 kilometres we had our first glimpse of the snow-capped Mount Ararat (16,800 feet), behind a lower range and which is supposed to house part of the remains of Noah's Ark. At 245 kilometres we rose into the Zagros Mountains and leaving Makon we were again stoned and found that our defensive/aggressive reaction was almost routine.

We arrived early at Bazargan, the border town by the Iran/Turkey border and, as we still had some unused coupons for free petrol provided by the Iran Auto Club, we filled up the tank. It was a mistake. As we queued with other competitors to exit the Iranian border our tank leaked like a tap. We hastily borrowed some more jerry cans - having ditched our plastic ones before Esfahan - and began siphoning off the fuel above the leak. The queue was on the move, however, and it was difficult to time the changing of the jerry cans. At one point Duncan was running alongside holding a jerry can under the siphoning tube as I drove the Delage slowly forward. We photographed and said goodbye to Preacher and other friends from the Iranian Auto Club and I paid Preacher for the cost of parts. He steadfastly insisted that his Club would pay for labour - another example of their warm generosity.

As we left the severely repressive society of Iran I found myself thinking about Britain with its new, young government. Whatever their political leanings I think that, across the board, British people would like to see the socialists do well and not fall on their faces. A country with at least two strong democratic parties is a healthy country. I do hope that Blair will be able to avoid being dragged by his left wing into over allowing for minority groups at the expense of the vast majority of ordinary electors. That could lead to Britain becoming too repressive, albeit any British government would fall on its face long before it reached the levels of repression evident in Iran. As we crossed the border we saw the first wasp we had seen since leaving England.

We went very quickly through Turkish Passport Control and Customs and I felt I needed to have at least a small amount of Turkish currency. The bank was closed and I exchanged with a shifty money-changer ten pounds sterling worth of Iranian cash for half a million Turkish lira. I found out later that he should have given me approximately twenty two million lira. Not a good start to Turkey but not exactly serious either. We still had 316 kilometres to drive to our overnight stay, a ski hotel in Palandoken, and at about 100 kilometres from the border and at a speed of almost 100 kilometres I nodded off to sleep. It was only a second or so but I awoke with a violent start and two wheels off the tarmac. It was not Duncan's time to drive but, showing generosity and self preservation, he took over for a while. In between dozing in the safety of the navigator's seat, I saw someone washing clothes in a river, what appeared to be peat cutting and a woman beating a carpet in the carriageway on our side of a dual carriageway. Soon we moved into a wide semi-fertile plain surrounded by mountains, some of which were snow-capped. Roadside turkeys again appeared before we cut into a beautiful, deep ravine with gorse covered sides. We joined the valley of the River Aras at Horosan and having covered 225 kilometres we stopped for petrol. That was when I discovered half a million lira was only worth 20 odd pence but, unfortunately, it was after I had put sixty litres in my tank. The attendant was, understandably, not warm or friendly. I offered to pay in dollars. Reluctantly he calculated for several minutes and then wrote on a piece of paper - $485. I indicated that I thought there was a one place decimal error, which he declined vigorously and now it was my turn to become less than warm and friendly. I needed to take him through the arithmetic before he finally settled for $48.50. Even that was about £2.50 per gallon.

With about 580 kilometres on the trip meter for the day we turned right as directed by the route book, only to discover when we became completely lost that it should have said 'left' (again). We were actually leaving Palandoken in the wrong direction on a dual carriageway when I sensed that it had to be wrong. I was too tired to risk driving way out of town before I found a place to do an 180° turn and so I backed up half a kilometre to talk to a policeman. He looked a little surprised but concentrated on re-directing me. On the right road once again, it was a very steep dirt road which led only to the Hotel Dedeman in Palandoken. Near the top we were in bottom gear and crawling so slowly I thought that the Delage would give up at any moment. She did not, bless her, she made it all the way up under her own steam. Several vintageant and classic cars had to be towed up the last two or three kilometres. Car 9 had also made it without help and Idris was indignant when the towed cars received no penalties for being towed. He was told they could not be penalised because they had not reported that they had been towed (some were towed by the rally back-up vehicle) and, in any case, the small print did not provide penalties for being towed.

Before submitting to the comfort of our hotel, Duncan and I discussed what to do about our persistently leaking tank. We decided to limp to Istanbul by filling the tank as regularly as possible to the level of the leak and use the filled jerry cans as back up. We would then either renew the tank at Istanbul or, failing that, limp to Paris. The hotel was like a breath of fresh air after Iran. The ladies looked ravishing after being so dourly over-covered in Iran. Drink was freely on sale and even cigars were available. To complete the ultimate contrast the hotel disco was in heavy demand. The relief was fairly short-lived however, as frost was forecast on our mountain road for the following morning and with a start time of 5.42am, we needed a 3.30am alarm call.

Chapter

14

We descended the dirt mountain road considerably faster than our ascent with the frost not causing great problems and we were soon in the long beautiful gorge of the fast flowing River Karasu. We had 739 kilometres to drive on our thirty-third day to reach Nevsehiv. After about 100 kilometres we saw much Army activity including an inverted car in a ditch being guarded by a tank and an active military observation post on a hilltop. We presumed that the activity was aimed at curbing or containing local terrorists. At 155 kilometres we were back on a wide plain with beautiful snow-capped peaks on the horizons to the left and the right. Thirty kilometres further on we stopped at a filling station to refill the tank about one-third full so that it remained below the leak. The attendant pointed to our rear nearside wheel - it had a ten inch split in the rim just below the spokes. In my view it was 'throw away' broken, and we exchanged it with the spare wheel. We drove on over 'bucking-bronco' roads along the silk route and under a cloudless sky. But our thoughts were not cloudless. In preparation for the rally we had replaced our old buckled wheels with five new wheels produced by the same supplier. What if another one broke in similar fashion - we would have to drive on three good wheels and one split one, which could disintegrate at any moment. Three wheels on my wagon and I'm still rolling along! We decided to telephone or fax that evening instructing that one of our old wheels be sent by DHL to us at Istanbul.

We entered Erzurum, the appearance of which belies its antiquity since it was largely destroyed by an earthquake in 1939. As we were leaving the route book directed us left but, fortunately, a policeman insistently directed us correctly to the right. On the outskirts we passed new European-style housing but soon we were into softer rolling hills with more coverage of trees. On the roadside were some large, heaped stores of what looked like turnips. After about 300 kilometres we drove over a peak of more than 2,190 metres and shortly afterwards we saw a truck carrying a military tank, which had driven through a barrier and down into a ravine. We arrived on time for the one intermediate time check of the day at Sivas, a very modern looking town in spite of its proximity to a settlement dating back to 2600 BC. At the time check Duncan borrowed the satellite telephone belonging to Idris and ordered delivery of our old wheel. He then treated me to fried chicken with good home-made chips. Our lunch used up a valuable twenty minutes but it was a worthwhile break. The roads became much smoother after Sivas but I still had the onset of saddle soreness and I longed for a modern, contoured car seat to replace the Delage seats which had back rests at a right angle to its hard seats.

We crossed a huge plain with a single road in the middle - the silk road - and as we passed through Sarkisla I saw a house with solar panels. 'What an untapped market.' I said. Soon we noticed that for the first time on the rally, we had bugs splattered on our windscreen. Now how does one explain that - no bugs on the windscreen east of Sarkisla? Some 80 kilometres before reaching Kayseri we drove into an area of much greater cultivation but there was still room between the arable areas for a shepherd mounted on a mule to herd his sheep. We noticed over a distance of many kilometres that every isolated dwelling seemed to be a small bungalow of standard design. There seemed to be no variation in either size or appearance. Had some Turkish entrepreneur cornered the market with a prefabricated design? Kayseri is a farming and textile centre leading to a plateau of soft, multi-coloured, stone called tufa and formed by a combination of lava, ash and mud when Mounts Evciyes and Hasan erupted three million years ago. The soft stone is so workable that many houses, chapels and monasteries have been hewn from it. As we left the area we were stoned once more at some traffic lights.

We passed close to Avacos, dating from the bronze-age, before reaching Nevsehiv, a modern town of historical origin, as confirmed by the ancient castle perched on a hill above and the Kusunlu Mosque. We arrived on time at 19.45 hours, but very tired, at the Dedeman Cappadocia Hotel. The management made us very welcome and we ate a substantial dinner. Jingers offered to weld our broken wheel if we could find welding equipment. I doubted whether any weld could possibly hold that split but we decided to countermand our instruction to send one of our old wheels. This was partly based on Francesca's experience of wasting four hours at an airport to achieve possession of a spare part. Her description of how she finally achieved possession of her spare part from customs officers displayed acting qualities which demand a leading role in a Hollywood blockbuster. Francesca's performance began with demands issued in strong authoritarian tones, but she admitted that she only achieved results when she burst into tears.

Before returning to bed - the next morning's alarm call was for 5.30am - we felt we had to go to the nightclub in the hotel and experience a display of the traditional local dance known as the Swirling Dervish. Their ability to spin without becoming dizzy and falling over was truly amazing but that apart, the performance was grindingly boring. I simply could not stay awake and I was asleep in my bed by 10.30pm. We started at 7.24am on the following morning, Thursday, 9th October. We had another long drive of 733 kilometres to reach Istanbul but at least it was another cloudless day. Soon we were into much more arable land with sandy red soil, some stubble burning and more large stores of turnips. We passed through Hacibektas where Onyx is widely found and Kaman with its nearby productive archaeological dig. Later we by-passed Ankara, the capital city of Turkey.

We arrived on time at the day's first time check in Golbasi but found that our rear mounted, beautifully crafted, mahogany tool box had burst open. We had to crudely nail and strap it together, much to Duncan's disgust as he had post-rally plans for the box. The second intermediate time check of the day was cancelled and so we set out to drive directly to Istanbul along the motorway. After a total day's distance of about 300 kilometres we saw Werner's Mercedes parked on the side of the motorway. He had a blow-out and was well on with changing the wheel but was worried that the spare was far too low and was laboriously working at his foot pump. He was very relieved when Duncan produced his battery operated pump and had it up to full pressure very quickly. Like us, Werner also now had no spare wheel.

The motorway cut through rugged hills and then back onto a wide plain but with all its undulations it is a surprising statistic that eighty percent of Turkey is 1,500 feet or more above sea level. Again, one feels that some enterprising entrepreneur has cornered the market with a standard design for minarets. Ninety-eight percent of the population are Muslim and so it is not surprising that the standard minarets, looking so much like missiles, were regularly seen on this section of our route. As we moved back into the hills again far more trees were to be seen, many showing autumnal colours. At 490 kilometres we pulled into a filling station and were soon in conversation with the proprietor, Nihat Abul. After many formal welcomes it was good to receive an unrehearsed, warm welcome from Nihat. He gave each of us a Coke and photographed us with the Delage. We exchanged cards and promised to write and exchange photographs. Soon we joined a toll motorway and after 90 kilometres of smooth driving at a cruising speed of 90 kilometres per hour, we passed Sapanca Lake, which has much of the tranquillity of Interlaken. Fifty kilometres more brought us to unremitting urban-scape with a great deal of polluting industry in a heavy pall of smog. It underlined how right Britain was to introduce the Clean Air Act in 1970 and how badly Turkey needs to enforce similar legislation now.

The industry became heavier with shipyards and a refinery accessible to both the Black Sea and the Aegean Sea. Increasingly, pockets of residential areas appeared with the apartment buildings now rising to ten storeys. As we drove down the four lane west-bound motorway leading to Bosphorous Bridge, young child vendors took advantage of the near grid-lock to peddle trays of drinks, sweets and flowers to the captive motorists. The vehicles were moving in staccato fashion with regular, opportunistic lane swapping. The children were running up and down, darting between the vehicles and if one were choosing a safe place for a ten year old child, that motorway would not have been in the first million selected. The slow moving traffic was further hindered by two rally cars, one of which ran out of fuel on the bridge whilst the air filter of the other caught fire. The River Bosphorous and the striking suspension bridge formed a beautiful foreground as the red sun sank in a sinister shroud of smog. The setting sun was picked up by occasional reflecting windows creating a form of urban beauty against a satanic cloak of pollution.

Close to the bridge we bought some sweets from the children and they shouted a joyful Gula Gula (Bye Bye). We checked in on time at 7.45pm at the Dedeman Hotel in

Istanbul which provided five star luxury. After dinner I telephoned my assistant and heard that my instruction to countermand the sending of the spare wheel was too late, it had already been despatched with DHL. I insisted that it must be delivered to our hotel as we would not have time to collect it. Duncan also telephoned his married, younger sister, Tanya, who did a valiant job of standing in for Duncan and providing direction to our company in his prolonged absence. Duncan had maintained regular, though not frequent, contact with Tanya and at one point he proudly showed me a fax she had sent to him. Nowhere in the fax were three words used if two were enough. The concluding sentence was a clear cut recommendation requiring merely a 'Yes' or 'No' from Duncan. We agreed that if Tanya chose to stay in commerce, she would go a long way.

Duncan and I concluded that we would need to work independently on the morning of Friday, 10th October, if our rest day was not to be totally swallowed up by work on the Delage and other preparations for the final leg of the rally. We were determined to be finished by lunchtime and to organise a private lunch where we would be hosts to competitors who had particularly befriended us. I described to Duncan my vision of a beautiful restaurant terrace overlooking the Bosphorous and after talking to the receptionist he suggested the Restaurant Iskele, a well regarded fish restaurant. I reserved a table for seventeen for 1pm and then spoke to fifteen guests inviting them and giving them a slip of paper confirming the time and place - it was the closest I could approach a formal invitation.

As filling stations were now much closer together, and also because we had realised that we could almost half fill our tank before it started to leak, Duncan and I decided not to attempt any further repair or replacement of the fuel tank, but to manage simply by filling it twice as often. In addition we thought we should buy some replacement, metal jerry cans and return the ones we had borrowed at the Iran border exit. I spent the rest of the morning chasing the wheel through the local DHL office and organising by telephone through Erman Akyörek, a member of the Turkish Rally Club, three metal jerry cans, a two tonne hydraulic jack and twenty four, two-inch wood screws. I offered to help in obtaining them or at least in collecting them but Erman insisted on delivering them to our hotel. I asked him if I could rely on him getting them to me. I think he was affronted by the question but he laughed and said: 'You can rely on me.' Duncan busied himself during the morning by adjusting our brakes and checking for loose bolts. He was assisted by two enthusiastic and cheerful stewards, Peter and Betty Banham, who hail from Alfreton in Derbyshire and who volunteered their help.

When we arrived at the Restaurant Iskele we were shown to our table. I was amazed that the terrace perfectly fitted my vision of the type of venue I sought. David & Pat Dalrymple, crew of a 1949 Cadillac Series 62 coupé, were already there and soon we were joined by Chris & Jan Dunkley, Adam Hartley & Jonathan Turner, David Bull, Angela Riley and Angela's mother, Helen McGugan, and Richard & Gill Dangerfield Unfortunately, Werner & Sylvia Esch, Francesca Sternberg and Jennifer Gillies, had to decline because their cars demanded their attention and so we were reduced to a table of thirteen. Francesca and Jennifer were replacing a universal joint and Werner was organising new tyres.

The service was impeccable and the wine flowed steadily. The head waiter addressed our party and suggested a mixed fish starter to be shared by all and various main courses. It worked beautifully and we all enjoyed an excellent meal. Everyone was in great spirits and, for me, it was one of the most relaxing events of the trip. The waiter brought what I thought was a very fair bill and when I asked about gratuities he asked if I would mind putting the tip on a separate American Express voucher. I felt that 20 million Turkish lira was an appropriate tip and thought that if one ignored the incredible exchange rate, then it could have justified an entry in the Guinness Book of Records.

Constantine the Great, the first Christian, Roman emperor transferred the capital of the Roman Empire from Italy to a little known settlement called Byzantium in the fourth century A.D. It was then called Constantinople and later still, Istanbul, the city where east meets west. To emphasise the meeting of east and west in the present era, Turkey's neighbour, Greece, is a member of the E.C., whereas Turkey would like to be a member. In Istanbul, the Blue Mosque, the Mosque of Sultan Suleyman the Magnificent, the Grand Bazaar, the Spice Market and the Topkapi Palace vie with each other for the attention of the tourist. This is a city I have to return to, in spite of the smog.

I managed a short siesta before the celebration dinner hosted by the Dedeman Hotel Group. BBC Radio Derby were supposed to 'phone me at 6.15pm for a short interview but no call was put through. Whilst the competitors were grateful to Dedeman for their hospitality, the dinner was rather embarrassing. They gave a number of well deserved prizes to some competitors but the razzmatazz and their obvious attempt to jump on the bandwagon, at the risk of stealing the glory of Paris, was clear. The glitzy performance reminded me of Neil Kinnock's vote losing event in Sheffield during the lead up to the 1992 British General Election .

We returned to our room at midnight contemplating the preparation we still needed to do and which we dared not leave till the following morning. Waiting in our room was a parcelled wheel from D.H.L., three metal jerry cans, a two tonne hydraulic jack and twenty four, two-inch wood screws. Erman had performed beautifully. Werner had also welded our split wheel and replaced its tyre and so we carried our new spares over to the car, put the split wheel back on as spare and tied the old wheel (without a tyre) to the rear, secure compartment. We were slightly nonchalant about securing the old wheel because, with a welded spare, we had been prepared to leave without the old wheel, if it had not arrived in time. We re-screwed the burst tool box but found that only two jerry cans would fit in and so we gave one new jerry can to a soldier who was providing security to the cars. We then arranged to return the borrowed jerry cans before leaving the following morning. We also ditched the old, damaged hydraulic jack.

Chapter

15

We rose at 5am to begin the third and final leg of our epic journey to Paris. Hermann (the German) Layher had recovered sufficiently from his hypothermia, followed by pneumonia, to re-join us with his 1907 La France for the last leg, albeit no longer as a competitor. Our start time was 7.03am and so we did not need lights and it was a dry, fine day but cooler. Driving out of the city it was evident that a huge amount of new building was underway, including many apartment blocks. There followed a great deal of holiday flats in the form of strip development along the coast road following the north shore of the Sea of Marmana. Not far south was the infamous Peninsular of Gallipoli, a name which persistently haunted and was the source of much anguish for Winston Churchill and the place where many ANZAC soldiers died in the First World War.

At around 160 kilometres we moved up into the hills and away from the coast and, 40 kilometres further on, we had reached a high plain of poor arable land with a green lake to the left. A policeman waved us down insistently but it was only to ask how many competitors were ahead and how many behind. As well as an unrelated patrolling hawk, there seemed to be increasing army presence. We arrived early at the Turkish Border but were allowed to report to the rally time check at 10.51am without penalty. We passed through Turkish and Greek controls very quickly in spite of a humourless Turkish passport official who was the ultimate, minor official indulging in the misuse of power. We zeroed our trip metre and set forth into Greece, soon to see a sign 'Welcome to the Country of Gods, Heroes and Civilisation'. It would make a good Labour Party slogan. At 15 kilometres we passed our first Western-style supermarket. At 40 kilometres we saw stubble burning and wondered why it is allowed in another E.C. country, but not ours.

It became very overcast as we drove into heath-land and forest, then soon back into poor arable land. Absorbing the agricultural scene was compulsive but, glancing at the map, I was reminded that Greece is, of course, a great maritime nation with the largest fleet in the world, even though its population is a mere ten million. Later we saw active cotton picking and later still in Xanthi we passed a stunningly beautiful lady strolling along the pavement. Leaving Xanthi we passed through an industrial area but by 200 kilometres we were in rocky hills near the coast. We stopped for a brief lunch of Greek salad and octopus at an open air café where we spotted some of our friends lounging under umbrellas. Soon afterwards we passed a sandy beach and then moved into a region of vineyards and orchards with a view of Mount Athos to the left. When we were crossing Asia earlier and eating too little, Duncan and I would have been very pleased to eat Mars bars. The only place where we found them was at a filling station in central Delhi, but now on our first day in Greece we found them again.

Even though we had left Asia behind we still saw a working mule and at around 325 kilometres a single flock of sheep. At 360 kilometres, industry reappeared on the approach to Thessalonika and we were surprised to see a beggar on the pavement's edge and pleased to note the absence of smog, as we arrived early, at 6.45pm, for our time check at the Makedonia Palace Hotel. We were not penalised for checking in early, having completed 640 kilometres in the day and we settled happily into our very comfortable accommodation. We should have enjoyed a view across the sea to Mount Olympus but the weather foiled us. Duncan and I took Werner and Sylvia for a fifteen minute taxi drive to be our guests at the Restaurant Maiami. We ate fish - 'Sole al fresco' - though we were able to eat inside, fortunately, as outside was torrential rain.

On Sunday, 12th October, we were due to start at 9.03am. Gerry Acher, the driver of a 1932 Aston Martin International with Bruce Young, presented all competitors with a letter. It suggested that we should all contribute to a fund to provide the hard working rally marshals and support staff with a momento of their essential contribution. A great idea to which we happily contributed. A second suggestion in his letter was that we should hold a general meeting that evening to discuss how we could all take part in giving charitable help to Nepalese children. Apparently he was touched by the smiling, healthy, young girls who greeted us at the Nepalese border, each bearing the famous Red Cross. I thought his second suggestion was ill conceived. It was too focused because we had seen far more desperate need on our journey across Asia and it was better tackled in our own country than in the thick of a rally.

After negotiating our way out of the city we joined an excellent dual carriageway, the National Road. The rain in Thessalonika was only the second downpour of the rally - how very fortunate - we had suffered extremes of weather but it could have been worse. We passed through Katerina and then up into beautiful, wooded hills along ever winding roads littered with hairpin bends, against a back-cloth of autumnal colours. The mule was still present even though we had left Asia well behind. We dropped down into a plain of poor arable land, with some pasture and the occasional flock of sheep, before rising back into the hills with tobacco drying in the roadside fields. Shortly after topping up with 60 litres of fuel, smoke billowing from our nearside rear wheel confirmed the brake had seized. We had to free that brake off completely to release it before we continued along car-killing roads. We needed to minimise our use of the brakes but it was an added hazard that, when we did need to use them, the brakes were unbalanced. The winding road threaded through the 'flying' monasteries of Metéora, dating from the 14th Century and housed in caves hundreds of feet above the road in near vertical rock faces. The only approach to the caves is by small baskets hauled up precariously on ropes, yet four of the caves are still occupied and this amazing arrangement was worked into a James Bond film. The bird's eye view of this staggering natural complex was rather obscured by heavy mist. We were twelve minutes late for one intermediate time check at Kalambaka where we stopped for a brief lunch.

Two cars emitted ominous noises as they left the time check. Don Jones, in car 65, stopped within a few yards to investigate the frightful, clattering noise from the rear of his Packard, as expectant fellow competitors looked on. Some wag had tied a tin can to his bumper! On sighting the offending can, Don's anxious expression was replaced in barely a second by his laughing relief. Prince Idris in car 9 took a little longer to establish that the jarring, metallic noise from the rear of his car was also the work of an unidentified wag. Someone had removed his hub cap and placed a large nut and bolt inside. Again, relief triumphed and Idris' laughter ensued.

We moved on through another huge plain of poor, arable land with some cotton fields and fringed with mountains. Then we passed through Artessiano followed by a scrappy industrial area, before reaching Kedros, our next time check, on time. We were allowed only one hour thirty two minutes to our next time check at Aghios Georgios and it was too tight a timetable for us so that we could only manage to arrive there seven minutes late. We passed through Thermopiles with its Lion Monument and Wall, proudly commemorating the resistance of the Spartans against the Persians in 480 BC, motoring on to arrive, on time at 19.43 hours, at the Hotel Astir Galini at Kamena Vourla for our thirty-seventh overnight stay.

Immediately after checking in we went out of our hotel for dinner at the Dolphin Restaurant as guests of the genial Adam Hartley. Werner was tired and went to his room on the second floor for an early night. He left the key in the door so that his daughter, Sylvia, would not need to waken him when she retired. When Sylvia went to their room she was amazed to find a man sleeping in each of the twin beds. One was her father and the other, a complete stranger. It transpired that the stranger had a room on the first floor and had mistakenly gone to Werner's room, on the second floor, and let himself in with the key left for Sylvia. In addition to being highly embarrassed, the intruder was very sleepy as he had been asleep in Sylvia's bed for three hours! We slept well and rose at 7am for a 9.03am start. The worst leg of the day had been cancelled, presumably because the rally office thought that many competitors would not make the boat in time and, apart from saving 200 kilometres of distance, it also removed some of the worst roads, which was a great relief after the beating our car had taken the day before. It was fine and warm and soon we stopped to take in the wonderful view through the Vale of Delphi. The weather became cloudy and blustery as we drove west into the hills and past many ancient battle sites. We skirted Athens but, regrettably, did not visit it. We made Amfiklia, our first time check, on time but then we negotiated a steep climb and descent with many hairpins and much nursing of our brakes, causing us to arrive six minutes late at Parnassos. We stopped and added 60 litres of fuel and drove on for about six kilometres when Duncan noticed that the top leaf of the front offside spring was broken. The jagged ends of the broken spring leaf had lifted and were clearly visible. We limped on to the next village, Livadia and pulled in to take a closer look. Tony Fowkes in a back-up Land Rover Discovery stopped to investigate and then monitored our progress by following us for about 20 kilometres.

We had passed many interesting tavernas en-route so when we reached our next time check, Kiato, early, we were dismayed to find that in order to avoid penalties we had to wait for thirty minutes. This meant having a MacDonald's lunch - only the second in my life - after passing endless tavernas. Tony Fowkes offered to put two metal straps on our broken spring and was soon joined by Duncan and several other mechanics thoroughly enjoying cosseting our defective spring. Tony thought the straps were, at best, a temporary measure and that during the coming sea crossing to Italy we should replace the straps with 3/8 inch plates. Jingers agreed with us that the straps might make it to Paris and perhaps even to our home in Derbyshire. We then had an easy ride to the Port of Patras along a dramatic coast road, the National Road, arriving early at the port to a distinctly festive atmosphere. In celebratory mood, Sarah Catt and Jasmine Lovric, a passenger in Car 38, rode on our running boards as we lined up for the ferry. I joined a party of high spirited competitors at the port café for iced coffee and Chelsea buns. Francesco Ciriminna, driver of Car 19, a 1948 Fiat, who was often serious and unsmiling was suddenly bubbling and laughing. Whilst sipping the coffee I was told the story of how one competitor, whose car was damaged and being transported by a truck back in China, was unable to find a seat in the vehicle and rode the whole journey sitting on a dead pig.

In the ferry queue, Adam Hartley and Peter Noble were needling each other to pass the time. Adam had removed Peter's much loved hat and soon a seemingly friendly but physically violent scrap ensued. It seemed dangerously violent and some of Adam's high spirits evaporated. We drove our cars in turn onto the ferry and Duncan and I privately decided not to attempt spring repairs during the voyage. The cabin was comfortable and, as neither of us is prone to sea sickness, we found the overnight voyage restful after days of tough driving. We ate a very acceptable meal of steak with a bottle of St. Emilion. Afterwards a high spirited Jane King, driver of car 82, bought a whisky for me. Jane was known as Rosie Thomas, her pen name as a romantic novelist. The sea was very calm and we slept well from about 1am, waking the following morning at 8.30am. It was overcast with the sea beginning to roughen. We enjoyed a leisurely breakfast with Francesca and Jennifer, sat chatting with Richard Dangerfield and David Bull for a couple of hours and then had a long, but light lunch of pasta with Richard Curtis. We had an extended siesta before a tedious wait to drive the car off the ferry and into Italy at Ancona, which dates back to the fourth century BC. We drove along a motorway in the dark to Rimini, which I had always thought of as no more than an Italian seaside resort but it dates from the third century BC. It was Tuesday, 14th October, our thirty-ninth overnight stay, only four days from Paris, when we arrived at the Hotel Continental e Dei Congressi in Rimini to be greeted by thunder and heavy rain. We taxied just 500 metres to a restaurant as Werner's guests for much better pasta than the ferry serving. Lord Montagu's Blower Bentley was delivered to Rimini to allow him to complete the last part of the rally and to reach Paris in triumph.

We awoke at 6.30am to start at 8.36am in fine dry weather. We were soon on steep, winding inclines with many hairpins on the way to the fairy-tale castles of San Marino, which has been an independent state continuously since the fourth century and so it is Europe's oldest state. The descent was very testing and I was consistently nursing the brakes. We had re-tightened the rear near-side brake after it seized and now it had seized again. Once more, we had to let it off completely so that it remained inactive for the rest of the day. Duncan became exhausted by the heavy toll of navigating in built up areas and so we exchanged places and continued, joining the Autostrada del Sole which passed through many fruit farms. We stopped for lunch at Galleria Ferrari in Maranello. Ferrari were celebrating their fiftieth anniversary year in 1997 and lunch was arranged at their Galleria. To my amazement they charged each person 28,000 lire (approximately £9.70 sterling) even though some of the competitors were likely to be Ferrari customers. Worse, the lunch they provided was meagre - cold meat and pickles - and way below the minimum standard which we would consider providing in our own company's name. In addition, some of the food had already run out. We scorned their meal and crossed to a small café on the opposite side of the road. I remembered my Larium tablet and took it late, with lunch.

When we left Maranello we were soon on narrow, busy 'bronco' roads where the locals seemed to believe that they could cut up visiting cars. Then we crossed the cheese and wine producing area of the infamous Po Valley with its mighty retaining banks, provided after disastrous floods, to try to keep nature in check. A motorway then took us around the majestic Lake Garda to our overnight stay at the Grand Hotel in Gardone Riviera. Sarah Catt was in playful mood when competitors arrived, spraying everyone with a water jet. The game was reciprocated, however, and she ended up soaked to her knickers! We checked in at 6.15pm and so, once again, I missed the suggested time for a BBC Radio Derby interview.

Chapter

16

Our forty-first day, 16th October, required us to drive for a mere 447 kilometres but it included driving through the Italian Alps, over the Passo di Resia and into the Austrian Alps. We rose at 6.30am for an 8.36am start in fine weather but with some cloud and a distinctly lower air temperature. Our exit on the west side of Lake Garda was along a picturesque, lake-side road with many period buildings and shows of still blooming, purple bougainvillaea. After Riva del Garda we climbed on a road cut into steep cliffs with many tunnels. Driving in and out of bright sunshine and tunnel darkness is an anathema for people who are prone to migraine, as I am, and so Duncan and I swapped seats so that he could drive. Moving away from the Lake we saw fairy-tale castles and towers ahead and passed by many vineyards. After about 80 kilometres we took the wrong autostrada access and had to retrace 5 kilometres to find the new Merano Autostrada. Although we were still over 100 kilometres inside the Italian border we increasingly saw signs in German and the architecture developed an alpine flavour.

We arrived at Resia on time at 13.25hours, though our lunch stop meant we were late re-starting. We negotiated the Italian/Austrian border smoothly and quickly descended through beautiful, alpine valleys with typical Austrian villages alongside a fast flowing, green river. We began climbing again to the famous ski resort of St. Anton and arrived at the Alberg Pass in sleet. We checked in on time at St. Christophe where a local vintage and classic car fan offered free, light food and a drink to competitors at the Arlberg Hospia Hotel. The descent was wet and slippery but as we left the snow behind, cows with cowbells tinkling grazed contentedly in luscious, green grass. We were just one minute late for the time check at Schwarzack. At the request of the marshals and along with other competitors, we took a black ribbon and tied it on our radiator to register our sorrow and sympathy regarding the death of Josef and René Feit, as we were soon to cross the border of their homeland. It was raining hard as we left and journeyed on to cross the bridge over the River Lieblach into Germany.

We had covered about 420 kilometres when our windscreen wipers began to fail with increasing regularity. Duncan was driving and he managed to restart the movement of the wipers after each stop by a sharp tap on the motor, at the top of the windscreen, with his clenched fist. Duncan's frustration with the recalcitrant wiper was in direct proportion to the strength of his 'taps' and suddenly after one forcible 'tap', the windscreen cracked in all directions, radiating from the wiper motor. Duncan was both angered and regretful by this worsening of our impeded vision. I maintained silence to avoid exacerbating what was already a further setback. The rain stopped briefly and relieved the tension.

Soon we were driving the road alongside Lake Constance and wondering aloud how such an idyllic, tourist-attracting area must have appeared so very different to the eyes of people desperately trying to escape from Germany to Switzerland during the Second World War. It began to rain again and we missed the final turning to our hotel, wasting twenty minutes in correcting our mistake and so we were fifty minutes late checking into the Park Hotel St. Leonhard in Uberlingen. Immediately after our arrival, Duncan repaired a leaking connection to the radiator and adjusted the wiper motor so that it was operating again. In doing so he somehow knocked out the power to the sidelights and fuel pump but, at this point, he decided to take a break and we enjoyed a good dinner with Richard and Gill Dangerfield. A special dinner was held in a private room adjoining the restaurant for the surviving family and friends of Josef and René Feit. Frau Feit had suffered an appalling, double blow and it seems that the dinner was cathartic for her. Competitors had been asked to add their own personal comment in a book of tributes to Joseph & René Feit. Our entry read: 'We feel profound sadness for the relatives of Josef & René Feit and that such an exciting event ended so tragically for them. Josef & René's contribution was to sustain the spirit of adventure. Nothing can take that away from them.' After dinner, Duncan and I returned to the car and Duncan soon restored the power to the pump and sidelights. However, during this operation we were approached by a strange Chinese lady who was clearly very interested in the Delage. She talked to us for minutes in Chinese leaving us no wiser, even her gestures did not help, and finally we conceded defeat and wished her 'Goodnight'.

We finally crawled into bed at midnight and awoke to the alarm, seemingly seconds later, at 5.45am for our 7.36am start. We were soon out of Uberlingen and into the rolling, mixed arable, pasture and woodland of the Black Forest. Patches of heavy mist made at least side lights necessary and I learned that Duncan's repair to the wipers had only succeeded in getting the driver's wiper working intermittently. After just over 100 kilometres we pulled into a filling station at St. Margan to top up with fuel. In the usual walk around the car looking for new things falling off, Duncan was shocked to see another ten inch split in the rear near-side wheel. It was the second wheel to split in this way and we exchanged it for the spare wheel - the original split wheel which Werner had welded for us in Istanbul.

As had so often been the case throughout the rally, the time spent exchanging the wheels neatly used up every spare minute of coffee time. The regularity with which running repairs squeezed out any suggestion of a leisurely lunch, or perhaps coffee whilst admiring a view, was very uncivilised. But we now had a new anxiety. Two of our five re-built wheels, installed as part of our preparation for the rally, had now failed in exactly the same place and with the wheel in the same rear, near-side position in both cases. If Werner had not welded the original split we would have been forced to take the tyre and innertube from the second split wheel and put them on the old wheel which had been despatched to us and which, with hindsight, arrived only just in time. Even so, if a third wheel split we would have to use the old wheel and a fourth split would reduce us to 'three wheels on our wagon'. At least, at that point, we were still rolling along and after checking in on time at Kandelpasshohe, we took in the panoramic views on both sides. Then we made a very steep, winding descent through forest, with Duncan nursing the brakes by using low gears.

In a wide, arable valley, interspersed with vineyards, we passed through the medieval towns of Emmendingen and Konigschaffhausen. Then over the River Rhine and into France where a huge river passenger cruiser was moored on the border. Twenty kilometres later we were on the 'Route du Vin' and passing through Alsace vineyards before reaching the time check at Riquewihr on time at 11.59am. Riquewihr is one of the many places the rally passed through which I intend to revisit. The competing vehicles were allowed to drive through the time warp of this ancient, wine village with its' cobbled streets, enclosing walls, arched Town Hall and Medieval fortress complete with a portcullis. The time check and lunch were at the Hotel Doler, built in 1547, in the main street.

About 100 kilometres further on we stopped to top up with petrol at Chatel sur Moselle and, on the inspecting circuit of the Delage, I groaned when I saw the welded ten inch split had opened up again. In spite of Werner's excellent welding job, the repaired wheel had lasted less than 200 kilometres. It confirmed what I thought from the outset, that a wheel so split was 'throw away'. We crept through the town seeking a repair garage but were turned away by a lady who made it clear that her men would be lunching or siesta-ing for some time. We crept on for another 5 kilometres and stopped hopefully outside another motor repair shop. This time we were welcomed and they soon put the tyre and innertube from the re-split wheel onto the old wheel, which we had so nonchalantly strung on the rear secure cover. The generous owner refused to take any payment for the work and so I rescued some packets of cigarettes from our baggage and distributed those. The cigarettes were originally intended to reward locals pushing us through rivers, perhaps in Nepal, but most of them had not been used.

Duncan resumed driving, nursing the car on a windy road through forest. We were both acutely aware that we were now just one more split away from having 'three wheels on our wagon'. About 70 kilometres after the second split, we passed through Aillianville with its XIth century fortress. Once again, I had become saddle sore. We were forty four minutes late arriving at Wassy and we set out on the final leg to Reims and were soon crossing a huge flat plain of mixed arable, pasture and woodland. We saw a large cereal factory with a railway siding in Songy and a pig farm at Coolus. We passed a majestic hawk sitting on a motorway fence and soon afterwards a windmill on the left was dramatically silhouetted against the sunset.

We arrived at the Hotel de la Paix in Reims for our forty-second and final overnight stay, before the finish of the rally. It seemed appropriate that Reims is known as the champagne capital. We were on time at 19.52 hours and we half-expected that our wives, who were staying in Paris, would surprise us and be waiting for our arrival in Reims. It was not to be, probably because of the complication of Sarah having two small children with her, even though her nanny, Felicity, was also with her in Paris. We dined with David Dalrymple, as his guests, his wife, Pat; Werner & Sylvia together with their newly arrived family, André, Werner's wife, and Katie, the six year old sister of Sylvia.

Chapter

17

We awoke at 7am for a 9.24am start and there was a great deal of excitement amongst competitors on that last day of the rally, Saturday, 18th October. The previous night was the only occasion on the rally when we had to put the Delage in a multi-storey car park and Duncan offered to go and recover it whilst I checked out of the hotel. Parking in the street adjoining the hotel was extremely difficult and Duncan decided to park with two wheels on the central reservation. He realised that he had mounted the curb too abruptly when he heard the metal straps on the front offside wing snap. I was anxiously trying to find the Delage so that it could be brought to the hotel entrance to load all of our luggage. When I did find the car it was surrounded by back-up mechanics with Duncan, who already had the car jacked up and the front wheel off. It was not the smooth start we had anticipated for the last day.

We still managed to leave on time and we had an unhurried three hour drive to Porte de Pantin. Duncan and I were excited about our fast approaching reunion with our wives and Duncan always disliked the very frequent route directions he had to interpret in a big city. In heavy traffic I questioned his navigation: 'Are you sure?' - in response to his correct direction: 'Fork right.' An angry exchange between us followed. It was only the third time in ten thousand arduous miles that there had been raised voices between us. We both thought that only three times in the whole trip was fairly good and at the end we felt closer than ever to each other but I was sad that the third one occurred within two hours of our final destination.

The Rally Association intended that the cars should leave Porte de Pantin to drive the final 11 kilometres to the finish in Place de la Concorde, in the winning order which marshals had finalised at Reims. Rumour and confusion contrived to defeat the intention and rally cars began to set off in random order. We followed Werner at quite a fast pace, dodging and slipping through heavy traffic which sometimes slowed to a snail's pace. We were speechless with anticipation as we drove along Les Quais de Rive Gauche with the River Seine and Notre Dame on our right, over Pont de la Conconcorde and into Place de la Concorde. The sight of our weeping wives made us feel emotional too. A few yards further on we came to a halt with kisses, hugs and tears of joy from our wives followed by Duncan's children, Oliver and Fergus, whooping with delight.

My daughters, Natalie and Tanya, Tanya with her husband Mark Spilsbury, my sister, June and her husband, John, hesitated just long enough for us to be reunited with our wives and then added their own special welcome. At one point a huge furry microphone was thrust over the steering wheel and into my face with a nearby T.V. camera focusing and an interviewer firing questions for the benefit of French viewers. I answered politely that our greatest emotion was relief at having made it to Paris but they soon realised that I wanted to turn my attention to my family and they left me in peace. The next wave of welcomes were from Sarah's nanny, Felicity, and mother and father, Michael and Bridgette Clifton. They were closely followed by our two engineers, David Whitehurst with his wife, Fran, and Simon Gibson with his wife, Angela. Duncan's friend, Michael Stevenson and his girl friend Amanda, made the total of the 'welcoming committee' up to eighteen people. Around us other cars were being mobbed by family and friends including Francesca and Jennifer who were locked in embraces with their husbands.

Wives and children clung to the Delage as we slowly manoeuvred into the secure area of parking reserved for the rally cars. I reversed into a space, switched off the engine and hurled the key over the bonnet into the crowd. An exuberant release of tension but not very practical. One of our group scrabbled around the feet of the crowd and recovered it. All competitors - but not their supporters - were invited to immediately attend a cocktail party in a nearby marquee. We had no intention of going anywhere without our families and so we declined and went for a light lunch and glorious beers in a small bar just off La Place de la Concorde. It had a narrow frontage but filled with our group there was a marvellous atmosphere.

We were reluctant to leave the bar but after forty-three days of commitment we did not wish to miss the final Gala Dinner. Finding a vacant taxi seemed impossible but then, as if from nowhere, a friend of David Whitehurst, Michael Shoobridge appeared with an Isuzu Trooper and saved the day. We showered quickly in our comfortable hotel, the Royal Monceau. In fact, we showered very quickly, because the one shortcoming of the Royal Monceau was that it ran out of hot water on the first evening of our stay. I changed into my dinner jacket and we took a taxi to the Hotel Continental. We gathered in the bar and we also joined with Jennifer and her husband, Gareth, for celebratory champagne.

The Awards Ceremony was held before dinner and began with dramatic excerpts from the official rally video. Phil Surtees and John Bayliss of Britain, drivers of a 1942 Ford Willys Jeep MB, took the prize as outright winners. The second and third places were taken by two 1950 Ford Club Coupés driven by Ted Thomas with Vic Zannis and John Jung with Andy Vann, all from the USA. The story was related of how a very sporting Ted Thomas had sacrificed the chance of overtaking the winner by stopping to help him with a clutch problem.[5]

Duncan and I had maintained throughout the rally our aim of simply getting the Delage and ourselves to Paris to be acknowledged as finishers. We already knew that we were to be awarded a finishers silver medal but, with the rally completed, we now knew that our two hour wait for our team car 12 at Tuotuoheyan was the only thing which prevented us from receiving gold medals. Even so we were both adamant that, in the same situation, we would do exactly the same thing. Having behaved in such an un-competitive manner we were totally surprised and grateful to hear that we had won cups for being third in our class. We were each presented with identical, impressive, silver cups. There is no great intrinsic value in such cups, but it was rewarding to have something tangible to remind us of our achievement in completing the longest motor rally ever.

The party was too big to dine in one room at the Continental and so we were allocated a series of tables for ten in three separate rooms. We were joined in the Napoleon Room by Nick Price, representing Norwich Union. We had also arranged for other rallying friends to be at other tables in the same room but, unfortunately, one party, Werner and Sylvia Esch and family, found that their table had accidentally been taken by Don Sneider's party. Werner had to move to another room and was very upset but Don Sneider and I managed to calm him and he settled in the other room.

The menu of

Crème de Faisan aux Chataignes

***

Selle d'Agneau en Croûte Dorée

Gratin de Courgettes au Basilic

***

Salade Gauloise

***

Assortiment de Fromages de France

***

Omlette Surprise Vésuvienne

***

Café

***

Wines

La Tour de Cluchon

Château Jean Gervais

lived up to the occasion and afterwards I sipped at a Montecristo No2. As we concluded a wonderfully satisfying day with a refreshing Harvey Wallbanger I said, 'Duncan, you're a hero.' Then I realised that anyone overhearing that remark would not rate my modesty, as I was on the same rally! Nevertheless, I believed it of Duncan and I did not dilute my remark to him. As we left, both of us with our wives and Natalie were faced with the prospect of a long wait for taxis when Richard and Louisa appeared with beaming smiles and offered to drive us to our hotels. Paris was proving to be quite a venue for taxi droughts thwarted by timely friends. We slipped into our luxurious bed at about 2.30am.

Irene and I awoke at 7.50am and spent a wonderfully relaxed hundred minutes talking contentedly about our separate activities for the last six weeks and our plans for the immediate future. A hundred minutes was not particularly long for our morning chats. I had just enough time after breakfast to collect the car, garage it at our hotel and taxi to Chez Francis, a typical pavement restaurant - the only way I wanted to lunch in Paris. Our family and friends met us there and, fortunately, it was a beautiful, warm, sunny morning. We had adjoining tables for twenty one people including Michael Shoobridge. It was a wonderful atmosphere and a memorable lunch. I felt I was enjoying a second honeymoon with Irene - or was it a third? Our one regret was that our Canadian friend, Tuppy Rogers, had to cancel his plan to join us in Paris because of his mother's sudden illness. However, Chris & Jan Dunkley, with Jan's two daughters, had chosen the same restaurant and it was good to see our team members lunching in relaxed mode. Before returning by taxi we looked at the wreaths for the late Diana, Princess of Wales, above the infamous underpass where she had tragically died and which was directly opposite Chez Francis. We siested till 7pm and had a light dinner with Michael and Bridgette. John and June had eaten separately but joined us for a drink after dinner and a very humorous conversation.

The alarm woke me at 5am on Monday, 20th October. It was like being on the rally again - almost. I recovered the Delage, loaded up and left with Duncan at 7am as I wanted to complete the round trip and drive the car back to my home in Derbyshire. There was no shortage of people offering to drive it back to England so that we could take a relaxed flight back to East Midlands Airport but I was determined to complete the loop and Duncan wanted to keep me company for the last leg. It was very foggy as we drove north from Paris using side lights and wipers as the fog was so wet. Soon the wipers gave up completely and so we pushed the roof back and, with a hand over the windscreen, worked the wiper occasionally. We drove straight on to the Tunnel's 11.51am train at Calais and arrived in glorious England in thirty five minutes. Glorious in that it was our beloved homeland - not in weather, which was similar to France. We set our watches one hour back, drove up the M20 and turned right onto the M25. We suddenly remembered that neither of us had any English cash. The toll office accepted ten French francs resignedly and with a wry smile from the operator. It was raining steadily and we found it was easier to lean over the windscreen and use a scraper rather than the wiper. I was reminded vividly of my early cars in my teens when I drove regularly without wipers and with just side lights. On one occasion, in my teens, when I had driven too fast through a large puddle in the dark, the car was discharging so badly I had to switch all of the lights off and switch them on briefly when another vehicle passed. Irene was my rear look-out telling me when a car was approaching from the rear. Happy days. We arrived at my home with a fine sense of achievement at 4.15pm, only one hour after Irene. We celebrated absolute completion with a bottle of Dom Perignon.

A Peking to Paris reunion at the Royal Geographical Society in London was organised for the 27th February, 1998. I would be away skiing in Switzerland at that time and so we resolved to hold a private reunion to include at least our guests in Istanbul. On 12th January, 1998, The Times reported an earthquake near the Great Wall of China, approximately one hundred and fifty miles North of Beijing. It was 6.2 on the Richter Scale and 50 people were killed, 11,439 injured and tens of thousands made homeless in bitter winter weather. My first reaction was a selfish one - how fortunate that our official start at the Great Wall of China was so timed that we were well away from the area when it happened. Then I began to think about the people whose normal lives are desperately deprived being hit by such a calamitous act of nature. How lucky we are to be born in this green and pleasant land where such disasters are unknown.

The Times of Friday, 16th January, 1998, included an article that gave me a vivid recollection of the Himalayas. It told the story of a young couple from Edinburgh who were on a two month trekking holiday in Nepal. They were in an area blanketed by deep snow after a two day storm, when they stumbled upon 25 Tibetan refugees, including some children, stranded in a blizzard. Members of the Tibetan party were in varying stages of frostbite and malnutrition. They had escaped from Lhasa and for three weeks had been heading for Kathmandu where they hoped Tibetan exiles would look after them. The conditions were harsher than they had expected and they did not want to risk approaching the Nepalese authorities and perhaps, being returned to Tibet to, possibly, face torture or execution. The British couple lead them through a 19,000ft pass and eventually to hospital. One refugee died, another had his legs amputated and several lost toes, but all those remaining joined in a grateful and tearful farewell when the heroic Brits flew home.

The Times of 19th January, 1998, reported that Iraq is raising an army of one million soldiers to wage retaliatory war if the United Nations do not remove their sanctions. This item followed only a few days after the reports of Iran's nuclear ambitions. Perhaps a greater danger to the West than the possible political threat in the form of Communist China, is the religious threat of Islam. One Iranian spectator told me that a Muslim could not rest until every human in our world became Islamic. Could it be the Crusades in reverse? Such thoughts seem far removed from the warm reception we received from each of the Asian peoples. Or could it be that the single Iranian, who made such a dire statement about Islamic conversion, is part of a tiny minority or holds an isolated view. Perhaps the bulk of Muslims recognise the extreme intolerance of the Crusades and follow 'In the name of Allah, the Merciful, the Compassionate'.

Chapter

18

I hope that this account has given you a strong feeling of what it was like to be behind the wheel of a vintage Delage on the World's longest car rally and for the kind of thoughts that were prompted by the events, the people, the beauty, the ugliness, the clamour and the serenity, en-route. As each day goes by Duncan and I are expressing growing, retrospective joy and satisfaction. I would like to have experienced a much higher proportion of 'enjoyment of the moment' during the rally. It is not my style to largely look forward and look back with enjoyment. I much prefer enjoyment of the moment. But we survived a tough rally and it did have some wonderful moments. If we had been allowed to enter a modern Ranger Rover the balance between enjoyment of the moment and retrospective joy and satisfaction would have been a much happier one - but that was not the deal.

Duncan and I have no regrets - we would not have missed it. One excellent bonus from the rally is that it provides a yardstick to use against every day problems and irritations. We keep reminding each other: 'Nothing is that important.' I am trying not to think about the next challenge - yet. But the spirit of adventure is alive and well.

END

APPENDIX 1 – RESTORATION

- Repair and re-fit radiator

- Remove engine and gearbox - strip engine and re-build

- Strip and re-build gearbox with new bearings and gears

- Design, manufacture and fit guards to the gearbox, fuel tank and sump

- Change speedometer head for modern-type kilometer and re-calibrate for accuracy

- Fit new brake linings to ensure brakes did full distance without being re-lined - harder material on the front than the rear,

- Re-set brake balance

- King-pins re-ground and new bushes made and fitted

- Assemble new prop shaft with new joints and flexible coupling to reduce shock loading to gearbox

- Making and fitting of new floorboards

- Assemble wheel bearing onto spare half-shaft

- Fit fuel bowl (water trap) with mounting brackets and pipework

- Clean and re-paint chassis

- Add secondary suspension to facilitate the carrying of 10cwt capacity on rough roads

- Design and manufacture framework for rear spares box

- Fit full exhaust system and re-design to give minimum of 8 inch ground clearance

- Remove rear axle, strip, inspect and re-assemble

- Overhaul the axle, including re-fitting of the exhaust system, rear springs, rear brakes and rear shock absorbers

- Re-manufacture new camshaft bearings, re-profile camshaft and re-face cam-followers

- Design and fit new purpose-built petrol tank to hold 38 gallons

- Re-line clutch

- 5 new wheels + 4 hubs resplined

- Shock absorbers

- Fit 2 new batteries

- Fit 2 battery boxes

- Design air intake filtration system

- Secure wiper blades

- Repair broken bonnet catch

- Repair hood frame

- Strip and re-build front and rear shock absorbers

- Remove steering box, acid strip, inspect, modify and re-assemble with new bearings throughout

- Re-design steering joint on drag link and track rod ends

- Remove rear seat to provide space for a purpose-built secure luggage box

- Re-condition leaf springs

- Drill chassis and fit front bump stops

- Remove halfshafts and differential - upgrade sealing to modern specification for pinion seal and inner and outer halfshaft seals to prevent oil loss. Modify housings to accommodate modern seals

- Water-proof all electrical components

APPENDIX 2 – OFFICIAL FINAL ENTRY LIST

Class V1: up to 3000cc

Class V2: 3001 to 4300cc

Class V3: over 4300cc

NO. ENTRANT / CO-DRIVER(S)	YEAR	MAKE & MODEL OF CAR	CC	CLASS
Vintageants Category (pre-1950 type)				
1 Lord Montagu of Beaulieu/Doug Hill (GB)	1915	Vauxhall Prince Henry	4000	V2
2 Hermann Layher/John Dick (D)	1907	La France Hooper sports	9400	V3
3 Walter Rothlauf/Fritz Walter (D)	1928	Bugatti Type 40 tourer	1496	V1
4 Gerry Acher/Bruce Young (GB)	1932	Aston Martin International	1493	V1
5 Gerhard Weissenbach (D)/Susanne Huslisti (A)	1928	Rolls Royce Phantom 1 boat-tail roadster	7668	V3
6 David Cohen/Adele Cohen (CDN)	1930	Stutz M Lancefield coupé s/c	5277	V3
7 Etienne Veen (NL)/Robert Dean (GB)	1927	Mercedes 630K sports	6200	V3
8 Kjeld Jessen/Hans-Henrik Jessen (DK)	1929	Bentley 4½-litre VdP Le Mans	4398	V3
9 Prince Idris Shah (MAL)/Richard Curtis (GB)	1932	Ford Model B saloon	3300	V2
10 Brian Ashby/Duncan Ashby (GB)	1930	Delage D8 drophead coupé	4050	V2
11 Charles Kleptz/Arlene Kleptz (USA)	1919	Marmon 34 Touring 4P	5700	V3
12 Chris Dunkley/Janine Dunkley (GB)	1935	Bentley 3½-litre open tourer	3587	V2
14 Baron Wilem Bentinck van Schoonheten (NL) Werner Hastedt (D)/Pieter Le Febvre (NL)	1936	Railton Straight 8 Fairmile drophead coupé	4200	V2
15 Don Saunders (USA)/Roger Coote (GB)	1932	Packard 903 convertible	6297	V3
16 Jonathan Prior (GB)/Mariam El Accad (D)	1936	Railton Cobham saloon	4168	V2
17 William Binnie/Edward Thompson (USA)	1928	Bentley 4½ HM sports	4500	V3
18 Francis Noz/Casper Noz (USA)	1928	Ford Model A roadster	3278	V2
19 Francesco Ciriminna/Michele Ingoglia (I)	1948	Fiat 1100 Cabriolet	1098	V1
20 Raymond Carr (USA)/Mike Wyka (POL)	1939	Ford V-8 convertible	4000	V2
21 Adam Hartley/Jonathan Turner (GB)	1929	Bentley 4½-litre VdP Le Mans	4493	V3
22 Pat Brooks/Mary Brooks (USA)	1949	Buick 59 Straight 8 Woody	4000	V2
23 Ted Thomas/Vic Zannis (USA)	1950	Ford Club Coupé	4000	V2
24 John Jung/Andy Vann (USA)	1950	Ford Club Coupé	4000	V2
25 Richard Clark/Ken Hughes (GB)	1948	Buick 8 Special Sedanet	4064	V2
26 David Dalrymple/Patricia Dalrymple (GB)	1949	Cadillac Series 62 coupé	5723	V3
27 David Arrigo/William Caruana (Malta)	1948	Allard M-type drophead coupé	3622	V2
28 Kurt Dichtl/Roswitha Dichtl (A)	1950	Rolls Royce Silver Dawn	4250	V2
29 Roby Hellers/Nicholas Thill (L)	1951	Sunbeam Talbot 90 drophead coupé	2267	V2
Touring Category				
31 John Stuttard (GB)/Roy O'Sullivan (GB)/ Simon Anderson (GB)/Gordon Barrass (GB)/ David Colvin (GB)/Robert Waters (USA)	1934	Rolls Royce 20/25 saloon	3669	-
32 Herbert Handlbauer/Elfi Handlbauer/ Lisbeth Handlbauer (A)	1938	BMW 328 sports tourer	1971	-
33 Joao Netto/Jose Costa Simoes/ Jose Machado/Jose Netto (P)	1932	Ford Model B saloon	3280	-
34 Bill Ainscough/William Ainscough/ Barry Attwood/Andrew Walker (GB)	1929	Chrysler 77 open sports	4300	-
35 Arnold Schulze/Jutta Breuer/Nora Schulze (D)	1950	Bentley Donnington special	6300	-
36 Jeff Fortune/Joan Fortune/Bud Risser (USA)	1955	Chevrolet station wagon	4000	-
37 Peng Yew Wong/Win Win Wong/ Suet Lyn Wong/May Lyn Wong (MAL)	1954	MGA sports	1800	-
38 Eustache Tsicrycas (GR)/Christoforos Karaolis (CY)/ Jasmine Lovric (CDN)	1955	Peugeot 403 sedan	1472	-
39 David Brister/Brian Miller/Keith Barton (GB)	1963	Rover 110 P4	2625	-
40 Mark Klabin (I)/John Dick II (USA)/ Jorg Holzwarth (D)	1964	Land Rover Series IIA 109	2497	-

APPENDIX 2 – OFFICIAL FINAL ENTRY LIST (continued)

Classic Category (1950 - 1968 type)

41	Burt Richmond/Richard Newman (USA)	1953	Citroën 2CV	602	C1
42	John Matheson/Jeanne Eve (AUS)	1967	Rolls Royce Phantom V	6250	C4
43	Johan Van der Laan/Willem Graal (NL)	1958	Citroën 2 CV	720	C1
44	Richard Sackelariou/Andrew Snelling/ Susan O'Neill (AUS)	1966	Wolseley 24/80	2433	C3
45	Jennie Dorey/Geoffrey Dorey (GB)	1960	Morris Minor	1293	C1
46	John O'Neill/Susan O'Neill-Tsicrycas (CDN)	1960	Volkswagen Cabriolet	1192	C1
47	John Thomason (GB)/Mike Kunz (USA)	1963	Triumph Vitesse	1596	C2
48	George Tinzl/Monica Tinzl (I)	1963	Peugeot 404	1618	C2
49	Lisa Klokgieters-Lankes (NL)/James Wheildon (GB)	1951	MG YB saloon	1622	C2
50	John Catt/Simon Catt (GB)	1965	Ford Cortina Mk1	1770	C2
51	Linda Dodwell/Genevieve Obert (USA)	1968	Hillman Hunter	1725	C2
52	Nigel Broderick/Paula Broderick (GB)	1967	Ford Anglia Estate	1680	C2
53	Maurizio Selci/Andrea Campagnoli (I)	1965	Citroën 2 CV	1299	C1
54	Werner Esch/Sylvia Esch (L)	1952	Mercedes Benz 300 B	3000	C3
55	Fred Multon/Tim Laughton (GB)	1955	Austin A90 Westminster	2912	C3
56	Peter Cordrey/Gordon Phillips (GB)	1961	Rover 100 P4	2625	C3
57	David Morris/Sheila Morris (GB)	1956	Austin A90 Westminster	2639	C3
58	Theodore Voukidis/Stelios Vartholomaios (GR)	1955	Chevrolet Bel Air	4000	C4
59	David Bull/Angela Riley/Helen McGugan (GB)	1965	Rover 3-litre P5 coupé	3000	C3
60	The Duke of Somerset/Anthony Hayes/ Christopher Shaw (GB)	1964	Ford Galaxie Country Squire	4699	C4	(Withdrew before the start)
61	Peter Noble/Susan Noble (GB)	1955	Bentley Continental Mulliner	4887	C4
62	The Honourable Francesca Sternberg/ Jennifer Gillies (GB)	1964	Volvo 122S Amazon	1800	C2
63	Erik Christiansen (Bahamas)/Philip Compton (USA)	1965	Rolls Royce Silver Cloud S3	4500	C4
64	Derek Radcliff/Nigel Webb (GB)	1953	Jaguar Mark V11 saloon	3400	C4
65	Carl Schneider/Don Jones (USA)	1954	Packard Straight 8 convertible	4000	C4
66	Renger Guliker/Gerda Guliker (NL)	1956	Chevrolet pick-up	3860	C4
67	Roberto Chiodi/Fabio Longo (I)	1964	Lancia Flavia coupé	1800	C2
68	Melissa Ong/Colin Syn (Singapore)	1963	Porsche 356 SC coupé	1600	C2
69	Daniel Orteu/Jonathan Davies (GB)	1962	Volvo P122S Amazon	1780	C2
70	Peter Janssen/Gunter Klarholz/Wolfgang Meier (D)	1965	Mercedes Benz 220A	2171	C3
71	Antonius De Witt/Herman Haukes (NL)	1964	Volvo 122 Amazon	1800	C2
72	Josef Feit/René Feit (D)	1967	Volkswagen Cabriolet	2300	C3
73	Werner Graf/Klaus Koppel (D)	1968	Triumph TR6	2467	C3
74	Friederich Flick (A)/Felix Mumenthaler (SW)	1964	Mercedes 220 SB	2200	C3
75	Bart Rietbergen/ Jolijn van Overbeehe-Rietbergen (NL)	1965	Volvo PV 544	2100	C2
76	Paul Minassian (F)/Paul Grogan (GB)	1962	Peugeot 404 sedan	1800	C2
77	David Hardman/Philip Dean (GB)	1964	Aston Martin DB5	3995	C4
78	Murray Kayll/Amanda Kayll (GB)	1967	Mercedes Benz 250 SE	2496	C3
79	Anthony Buckingham/Simon Mann (GB)	1964	Aston Martin DB5	3997	C4
80	Thomas Noor (D)/Maria Bouvier-Noor (F)/ Henning Kohler (D)	1966	Mercedes Benz 250 SEC	2496	C3
81	John Goldsmith/Murdoch Laing (GB)	1966	Aston Martin DB6	4200	C4
82	Jane King/Phil Bowen (GB)	1968	Volvo 122 Amazon	1986	C2
83	David Wilks/Andrew Bedingham (GB)	1974	Austin 1800 saloon	1800	C2
84	Ivar Moe/Tom Granli (N)	1969	Morgan Plus 8 sports	3500	C4
85	Seyed Amir Ali Javed/ Homayoun Kamal Hedayat (Iran)	1970	Peykan Hunter saloon	1725	C2
86	Vahid Kazerani/Roozben Razzaghi (Iran)	1970	Peykan Hunter saloon	1725	C2
87	Mohsen Eijadi/Ramin Khadem (Iran)	1970	Peykan Hunter saloon	1725	C2
88	Gerald Crown/John Bryson (AUS)	1964	Holden EH saloon	3300	C4
89	Anton Aan de Stegge/Willemien Aan de Stegge (NL)	1966	Citroën ID 21	2300	C3
90	Richard Dangerfield/Jill Dangerfield (GB)	1965	Holden HR saloon	3500	C4
91	Howard Bellm/Christopher Taylor (GB)	1968	Chevrolet Camaro	5740	C4
92	Rolf Mayer/Gerrit Geiser (D)	1968	Mercedes Benz 280SE	2800	C3
93	Jonathan Lux/David Drew (GB)	1972	Rover 3.5 P5B coupé	3500	C4

Classic 4-Wheel Drive Category

96	Nigel Challin/Anthony Jefferis (CD)	1955	Land Rover Series 1	1997	-
97	John Bayliss/Phil Surtees (GB)	1942	Ford Willys Jeep MB	2199	-
98	Carolyn Ward/David Tremain (GB)	1961	Land Rover Series 11A	2286	-
99	Richard Taylor/Larry Davis/David Pierce (USA)	1962	Willys Jeep Station Wagon	3870	-

APPENDIX 3 – SPARES AND TOOLS

- Half shaft
- Front & rear wheel bearings and seals
- Prop shaft, universal joint repair kit + roto flex coupling
- 6 fuel filters
- 4 carburettor repair kits
- 2 carb/accelerator return springs
- Radiator hoses (set) and hose clips
- 2 exhaust valves
- Radiator cap (aluminium)
- Water pump
- 2 fan belts
- 2 H.T. leads to fit longest application
- Distributor cap
- 1 rotor arm
- 1 condenser
- 2 pairs of points/contacts (LH & RH)
- 8 spark plugs
- Fuses + bulbs (replacement for every application)
- Dynamo brushes + "V.W. Beetle" regulator control box
- 2 wiper blades
- Electrical wire and connectors
- Cylinder head gasket
- Plastic metal
- Silicone glue (instant gasket)
- 2 spare wooden shock absorber discs
- 2 spare metal shock absorber discs
- 1 brake cable + 'D' clamps
- Octane booster
- Tank tape and PVC insulation tape

- Cable ties (assorted)
- Locking wire
- Radseal
- Selection nuts/bolts/washers
- Copper/fibre washers + PTEFE tape
- Tow rope
- Puncture repair kit + cold vulcanising patches
- Foot type pump
- Electric type pump
- Torch and batteries
- Plastic sheet
- Funnel with filter + nylon stocking
- 2 tins RPM + 1 tin WD40
- 17 piece socket set
- 6 pairs pliers
- Punches
- Torque/cracker bar
- Half shaft puller
- Box spanner (for rear hub nuts)
- Super glue
- 2 Tip Top repair aerosol cans
- 3 litres 140 oil (gear & rear axle)
- 1 litre anti-freeze
- Volt meter
- 4 Hot Cans
- 2 axle stands
- Earth strap
- Surgical gloves
- Carb needles + jets
- Stanley knife + pen knife
- Insulation tape

APPENDIX 3 – SPARES AND TOOLS (continued)

- 20 spanners
- Hammer
- 1 pair snips
- Socket box
- 2 hub pullers (to remove brake drums)
- Flexible grease gun + tin x RG2
- Grease nipple converter
- Copper slip grease
- 5 litres engine oil (20/50)
- Water purifying tablets
- 20 one litre bottles of drinking water
- Tyre + 5 inner tubes (1 new + 4 old)
- 4 snow chains
- Tyre pressure gauge
- Tyre irons
- Tyre beadbreaker
- Silicone spray
- Feeler gauge
- Points stone
- Dusters / non-lint cloths
- Marker pens

- Starting handle
- Fuel hose
- Terminals + clips
- Exhaust clamp
- Flexible repair section for exhaust
- Hand wipes
- Metal saw
- Allen key set
- 6 screwdrivers
- 2 adjustable spanners
- Cap spanner
- 2 tyre levers
- Jacking board
- Route card board
- Inspection light (12 volt)
- Containers of:

  Nuts

  Bolts

  Electrical connectors, etc
- 2 one gallon metal petrol can

APPENDIX 4 – OFFICIAL RESULTS AT TIME CHECK 99 - PARIS

Medal	Rally No.	Crew	Car	Class	Total Penalty	Position Overall	Class
Gold	97	Surtees / Bayliss	Ford Willys Jeep MB	6	43d 0h17	1	1
Gold	23	Thomas / Zannis	Ford Club Coupé	1	43d 0h21	2	1
Gold	50	Catt / Catt	Ford Cortina MkI	3	43d 0h44	3	1
Gold	24	Jung / Vann	Ford Club Coupé	1	43d 0h53	4	2
Gold	88	Crown / Bryson	Holden EH saloon	5	43d 0h55	5	1
Gold	52	Broderick / Broderick	Ford Anglia Estate	3	43d 0h59	6	2
Gold	85	Javed / Hedayat	Peykan Hunter saloon	3	43d 1h42	7	3
Gold	87	Eijadi / Khadem	Peykan Hunter saloon	3	43d 2h08	8	4
Gold	28	Dichtl / Dichtl	Rolls Royce Silver Dawn	2	43d 2h12	9	1
Gold	86	Kazerani / Razzaghi	Peykan Hunter saloon	3	43d 2h15	10	5
Gold	77	Hardman / Dean	Aston Martin DB5	5	43d 2h18	11	2
Gold	78	Kayll / Kayll	Mercedes Benz 250 SE	4	43d 2h19	12	1
Gold	90	Dangerfield / Dangerfield	Holden HR saloon	5	43d 2h30	13	3
Gold	98	Ward / Tremain	Land Rover Series IIA	6	43d 2h56	14	2
Gold	48	Tinzl / Tinzl	Peugeot 404	3	43d 3h26	15	6
Gold	21	Hartley / Turner	Bentley 4½-litre VdP Le Mans	2	43d 3h30	16	2
Gold	44	Sackelariou / Snelling / O'Neill	Wolseley 24/80	4	43d 3h44	17	2
Gold	47	Thomason / Kunz	Triumph Vitesse	3	43d 3h59	18	7
Gold	80	Noor / Bouvier-Noor	Mercedes Benz 250 SEC	4	43d 4h07	19	3
Gold	82	King / Bowen	Volvo 122 Amazon	3	43d 4h18	20	8
Silver	43	Van der Laan / Graal	Citroën 2CV	1	43d 4h29	21	3
Silver	92	Mayer / Geiser	Mercedes Benz 280SE	4	43d 4h30	22	4
Gold	41	Richmond / Newman	Citroën 2CV	1	43d 4h42	23	4
Gold	74	Flick / Mumenthaler	Mercedes 220 SB	4	43d 5h17	24	5
Gold	69	Orteu / Davies	Volvo P122S Amazon	3	43d 5h27	25	9
Gold	26	Dalrymple / Dalrymple	Cadillac Series 62 coupé	2	43d 5h39	26	3
Silver	58	Voukidis / Vartholomaios	Chevrolet Bel Air	5	43d 5h55	27	4
Gold	71	De Witt / Haukes	Volvo 122 Amazon	3	43d 5h58	28	10
Gold	53	Selci / Campagnoli	Citroën 2CV	3	43d 6h16	29	11
Silver	57	Morris / Morris	Austin A90 Westminster	4	43d 6h35	30	6
Gold	17	Binnie / Thompson	Bentley 4½ HM sports	2	43d 6h55	31	4
Gold	51	Dodwell / Obert	Hillman Hunter	3	43d 6h57	32	12
Silver	55	Multon / Laughton	Austin A90 Westminster	4	43d 7h43	33	7
Silver	76	Minassian / Grogan	Peugeot 404 sedan	3	43d 8h17	34	13
Silver	20	Carr / Wyka	Ford V-8 convertible	1	43d 9h03	35	5
Silver	19	Ciriminna / Ingoglia	Fiat 1100 Cabriolet	1	43d 10h18	36	6
Silver	91	Bellm / Taylor	Chevrolet Camaro	5	43d 10h22	37	5
Silver	73	Koppel / Kuhn	Triumph TR6	4	43d 10h24	38	8
Silver	62	Sternberg / Gillies	Volvo 122S Amazon	3	43d 10h35	39	14
Silver	49	Klokgieters-Lankes / Wheildon	MG YB saloon	1	43d 12h20	40	7
Silver	99	Taylor / Davis / Pierce	Willys Jeep Station Wagon	6	43d 13h30	41	3
Silver	75	Rietbergen / van Overbeehe-Rietbergen	Volvo PV 544	4	43d 15h53	42	9
Silver	54	Esch / Esch	Mercedes Benz 300 B	4	43d 15h55	43	10
Silver	68	Ong / Syn	Porsche 356 SC coupé	3	43d 15h59	44	15
Silver	10	Ashby / Ashby	Delage D8 drophead coupé	1	43d 20h36	45	8
Silver	9	Idris Shah / Curtis	Ford Model B saloon	1	43d 21h07	46	9
Silver	12	Dunkley / Dunkley	Bentley 3½-litre open tourer	1	44d 2h02	47	10
Silver	59	Bull / Riley / McGugan	Rover 3-litre P5 coupé	4	44d 3h16	48	11
Silver	8	Jessen / Jessen	Bentley 4½-litre VdP Le Mans	2	44d 4h14	49	5
Silver	14	Bv. Schoonheten / Hastedt / Ellison	Railton Straight 8 Fairmile drophead coupé	2	44d 5h13	50	6
Silver	4	Archer / Young	Aston Martin International	1	44d 12h07	51	11
Silver	67	Chiodi / Longo	Lancia Flavia coupé	3	45d 4h19	52	16
Bronze	83	Wilks / Bedingham	Austin 1800 saloon	3	45d 5h08	53	17
Bronze	89	Aan de Stegge / Aan de Stegge	Citroën ID21	4	45d 6h52	54	12
Bronze	65	Schneider / Jones	Packard Straight 8 convertible	5	45d 17h23	55	6
Bronze	39	Brister / Barton	Rover 110 P4	4	45d 17h55	56	13
Bronze	42	Matheson / Eve	Rolls Royce Phantom V	2	48d 16h15	57	7
Bronze	7	Veen / Dean	Mercedes 630K sports	2	49d 2h38	58	8
Bronze	81	Goldsmith / Laing	Aston Martin DB6	5	49d 17h15	59	7
Bronze	27	Arrigo / Caruana	Allard M-type drophead coupé	1	50d 8h53	60	12

Medal	Rally No.	Crew	Car	Class	Total Penalty	Position Overall	Class
Bronze	64	Radcliff / Webb	Jaguar Mark VII saloon	5	50d 11h34	61	8
Bronze	70	Janssen / Klarholz / Meier	Mercedes Benz 220A	4	50d 13h45	62	14
Bronze	16	Prior / El Accad	Railton Cobham saloon	2	51d 13h51	63	9
Bronze	56	Cordrey / Phillips	Rover 100 P4	4	52d 9h51	64	15
Bronze	25	Clark / Hughes	Buick 8 Special Sedanet	1	54d 12h06	65	13
Bronze	79	Buckingham / Mann	Aston Martin DB5	5	55d 10h58	66	9

Individual Touring Category

	Rally No.	Crew	Car	Class	Total Penalty	Position Overall	Class
	93	Lux / Drew / Shaw	Rover 3.5 P5B coupé	7	43d 0h01	-	1
	36	Risser / Fortune / Wilson / Risser	Chevrolet station wagon	7	43d 1h50	-	2
	37	Wong / Wong / Wong / Wong	MGA sports	7	43d 2h08	-	3
	35	Schulze / Breuer / Schulze	Bentley Donnington special	7	43d 18h01	-	4
	40	Klabin / Dick II / Holzwarth	Land Rover Series IIA 109	7	44d 0h42	-	5
	46	O'Neill / O'Neill-Tsicrycas	Volkswagen Cabriolet	7	45d 8h33	-	6
	3	Rothlauf / Walter	Bugatti Type 40 tourer	7	46d 9h58	-	7
	38	Tsicrycas / Karaolis / Lovric	Peugeot 403 sedan	7	48d 4h40	-	8
	31	Stuttard / O'Sullivan / Anderson / Barrass	Rolls Royce 20/25 saloon	7	48d 23h14	-	9
	29	Hellers / Thill	Sunbeam Talbot 90 drophead coupé	7	49d 10h48	-	10
	45	Dorey / Dorey	Morris Minor	7	51d 2h26	-	11
	32	Handlbauer / Handlbauer / Handlbauer	BMW 328 sports tourer	7	53d 2h30	-	12
	63	Christiansen / Veys	Rolls Royce Silver Cloud S3	7	54d 0h52	-	13
	34	Ainscough / Ainscough / Attwood	Chrysler 77 open sports	7	55d 0h01	-	14
	61	Noble / Noble	Bentley Continental Mulliner	7	62d 23h00	-	15
	15	Saunders / Coote	Packard 903 convertible	7	64d 7h45	-	16

Retired:

	Rally No.	Crew	Car	Class	
	84	Moe / Granli	Morgan Plus 8 sports	5	Retired - Engine
	5	Weissenbach / Huslisti	Rolls Royce Phantom I boat-tail roadster	2	Retired
	96	Challis / Jefferis	Land Rover Series I	6	Retired - Off Road
	66	Guliker / Guliker	Chevrolet pick-up	5	Retired
	2	Layher / Dick	La France Hooper sports	2	Retired - Illness
	22	Brooks / Brooks	Buick 59 Straight 8 Woody	1	Retired - Engine
	6	Cohen / Cohen	Stutz M. Lancefield coupé s/c	2	Retired - Electrics
	1	Lord Montagu / Hill	Vauxhall Prince Henry	1	Retired - Overheating
	11	Kleptz / Kleptz	Marmon 34 Touring 4P	2	Retired - Axle
	18	Noz / Noz	Ford Model A roadster	1	Retired - Engine
	33	Netto / Simoes / Machado / Netto	Ford Model B saloon	7	Retired - Engine

OTHER BOOKS BY THE SAME AUTHOR:

WHO GOES THERE?
Paperback novel : 1996 : ISBN 1-900686-007

Richard Moore has progressed from his wild, undergraduate days and become a nationally respected neuro-radiologist and one of Toronto's most eligible bachelors. But beneath the facade, he is deeply troubled by the burden of debt which began at university and spiralled with his penchant for high living linked with accidents of fortune.

He introduces a British friend to a $270 million office development in downtown Toronto, in the hope of solving his own money problems at a stroke, by taking a small slice of the projected multi-million dollar profit. But will it solve his problem, or will the evil influence of the Toronto Mafia bring disaster to him and his friend?

The key to his survival is to anticipate the answer to the eternal human question -

"Who goes there, friend or foe?"

❧

THE ADVENTURES OF LARAGON
Children's fiction : 1996 : ISBN 1-900686-01-5

Once upon a time, there was a little boy named Laragon.

So begin ten magical, short stories which lift the imagination of children beyond everyday life.

Adults reading them to children could hear a pin drop.

Children will read them again and again